C000075663

Management Skills: A Resource-Based Approach

for the Hospitality and Tourism Industries

Sally Messenger Rob Allen

Cassell
Villiers House
41/47 Strand
London WC2N 5JE.

387 Park Avenue South
New York
NY 10016-8810.

First published 1994.

British Library Cataloguing-in-Publication Data
A catalogue record for this book is available from the British Library.
ISBN 0 304 - 32924 - X

Typeset by Richard Teare
Printed and bound in Great Britain by Hollen Street Press, Berwick-upon-Tweed.

Current Titles in the Hospitality and Tourism Resource-Based Series:

Series Editor: Professor Richard Teare

- Strategic Management
- Marketing Management
- Operational Techniques
- Operations Management
- Management Skills

INTRODUCTION

OVERVIEW

As hospitality and tourism organizations de-layer and restructure, the role of the manager is being questioned. Charles Handy anticipates that in the future managers will not be required to direct and control others but instead will need to be able to develop staff and facilitate teamwork - in essence moving towards a more supportive role.

Why a resource-based approach?

The concept of a resource-based approach to human resource management and more specifically, management skills, is centred on the need for a pragmatic, problem-solving orientation. Accordingly, the book draws from a number of existing publications in order to provide an affordable, easy-to-use guide to industry applications and examples.

Readership

A key consideration in the book's design and layout is flexibility of use. It is intended as a core text for courses at undergraduate level, as a resource for open/distance learning courses and short course programmes and as a convenient, easy-to-use reference guide for managers working at all organizational levels, and in both operational and specialized roles. To ensure continued relevance, the format of the book allows for updating and extension.

APPROACH

Introduction

Each chapter begins with an introductory overview of the topic, followed by a contents list and related reading references which can be found in the resource publications. Access to all of the listed publications is strongly recommended.

Review

The chapter review provides a summary of key issues, influences and changes relating to the topic area. Where appropriate, industry examples are used to illustrate how hospitality/tourism firms might adapt existing practices.

Conclusion and extension

A concluding statement is followed by a series of review questions which relate to the key points raised in the chapter. In most cases, the review questions test comprehension of the topic material and relevant application by requiring the reader to draw from his or her industry observations and experience. All of the extension questions and exercises are linked to people and business case issues.

Teaching and learning

It is my view that the resource-based approach is flexible enough to support and encourage a range of different teaching and learning activities. These include:

(a) Reader-centred, independent study and investigation, including some self-assessment using the review and extension material. In this situation the teacher facilitates the learning activity through tutorial discussion, workshop activity and group project work involving discussion, debate and presentations, among other interactive techniques.

(b) Resource material for open/distance learning courses whereby the reader works independently at his/her own pace to an agreed learning contract. The review and extension material is suitable for self-assessment and for seminar and syndicate work whenever course meetings take place.

(c) Specific focusing on business practices and personal development applications in hospitality/tourism organizations, perhaps as part of a wider focus on the service industry sector.

(d) As a resource for the cross-fertilization of ideas and practices, especially in relation to the way in which the extension material is used.

Summarizing, the book can be used to facilitate independent learning, direct aspects of self-assessment and to support an array of individual, group project and interactive seminar and workshop activities.

I would like to thank Sally Messenger and Rob Allen for their valued contribution to the resource-based series and the series publisher, Judith Entwisle-Baker.

Richard Teare
Series Editor

CONTENTS

RATIONALE

In order to be an effective manager in the hospitality/tourism industries it is necessary to understand people - how they behave and the approach they take towards their work. Before an individual can begin to understand others they need to appreciate their own differences, perceptions and abilities so as to develop working relationships.

Managing staff also requires the development of communication skills to facilitate the flow of information that organizations need to function. Developing teams and motivating people demands good interpersonal skills; based on a knowledge and understanding of human behaviour.

The ability to plan and organize is an essential requirement for managers in today's hospitality/tourism industries. With the drive towards productivity, efficiency and the control of costs, more emphasis is being placed on how managers use their time and the results they achieve.

More attention is also being given to the development of decision-making and problem solving skills. With increased pressure to meet performance targets and more demanding and discerning customers, difficult situations may arise. As a result, managers have to cope with conflict, stress and anger. So in the future, hospitality and tourism managers will need a high level of personal and interpersonal skill so as to respond to the challenges of the next decade.

RESOURCES

The following publications constitute the resource on which this book is based:

A   R. Nelson-Jones, *Effective Thinking Skills: Preventing and Managing Personal Problems.* Cassell, London & New York, 1989. Pb. £14.99 ISBN 0-304-31719-5.

B   R. Nelson-Jones, *Lifeskills: A Handbook.* Cassell, London & New York, 1991. Pb. £14.99 ISBN 0-304-32396-9.

C   R. Nelson-Jones, *Human Relationship Skills.* Cassell, London & New York, 1992. Pb. £15.99 ISBN 0-304-31962-7.

D   A. Lockwood & P. Jones, *People and the Hotel and Catering Industry.* Cassell, London & New York, 1992. Pb. £14.99 ISBN 0-304-31511-7.

E   D. Evans, *Supervisory Management.* Cassell, London & New York, 1993. Pb. £14.99 ISBN 0-304-32296-2.

F   A. Murdock and C. Scutt, *Personal Effectiveness.* The Institute of Management & Butterworth-Heinemann, Oxford, 1993. Pb. £14.95 ISBN 0-7506-0665-7.

G   L. J. Mullins, *Hospitality Management: A Human Resources Approach.* Pitman, London, 1992. Pb. £16.99 ISBN 0-273-03395-6.

- *International Journal of Contemporary Hospitality Management* (IJCHM) MCB University Press, Bradford, Yorkshire, UK. ISSN 0959-6119 (published seven times a year).

Additionally:

- *International Journal of Hospitality Management* (IJHM) Pergamon Press, Oxford, UK.

- *Cornell Quarterly,* Cornell University, Ithaca, USA.

All references to the resource publications are cited in abbreviated form. For example:

- Chapter 2 in *Effective Thinking Skills: Preventing and Managing Problems* is cited as A: 2 pp 13-23.

- Articles published in the *International Journal of Contemporary Hospitality Management* are cited by author, volume, number, year, and page number(s) e.g. M.D.Olsen, IJCHM, v1n2, 1989 p.6.

We would like to express our thanks to Stephanie, Christopher and Joel Cadbury-Allen and to Ron and Win Messenger for their love and support. We would also like to thank Andrea West for her hard work in typing much of the intial draft and Richard Teare for his encouragement, support and invaluable help in preparing the final manuscript.

Sally Messenger and Rob Allen
September, 1994

Sally Messenger is Lecturer in Hotel Management, Department of Management Studies, University of Surrey. She has extensive experience of designing competence-based qualifications and has co-authored and co-edited several books on hospitality management topics.

Rob Allen is a Senior Lecturer in the Department of Service Industries, Bournemouth University. He currently specializes in teaching and learning concerned with personal effectiveness. He is an economist by training and has also taught tourism studies in recent years.

1
DIFFERENCES

INTRODUCTION

"A tortoise carries a stranded scorpion across a river. The scorpion stings the tortoise, who demands indignantly, 'My nature is to be helpful. I have helped you and now you sting me.' 'My friend', says the scorpion, 'Your nature is to be helpful. Mine is to sting. Why do you seek to transform your nature into virtue, and mine into villainy?'" Idnes Shah, *The Commanding Self.* Octagon Press, London, 1994.

Why is it important for managers of hospitality and tourism organizations to be aware of individual differences? There are three main reasons. First, so that they become sensitive to how their own personality interacts and affects other people, such as staff, clients and customers. It is, in other words, a starting point for self-management. Second, managers have to utilize the intelligence of their staff in such a way as to maximize productivity, while at the same time providing them with opportunities for self-development and advancement. Understanding individual differences then, is an important aspect of managing others. Third, managers must strive to fulfill the organization's objectives,and satisfy customers, clients, shareholders and external agents. Understanding individual differences therefore facilitates managerial work.

In this chapter:
- Individual differences and behaviour
  (A: 10 pp 154 -177; C: 2 pp 21-55;
  C: 3 pp 56-86; D: 2 pp 13-28)
- Analyzing individual differences
  (D: 2 pp 11-28)(2)
- Implications for managers of hospitality and tourism organizations (D: 2 pp 11-28)

REVIEW

Individual differences and behaviour
(A: 10 pp 154-177; C: 2 pp 21-55; C: 3 pp 56-86; D: 2 pp 13-28)
Each individual has characteristics that reflect both genetic (natural) and cultural, social and environmental (nurtured) influences. The most important differences relate to: (a) physical characteristics; (b) intelligence and (c) personality.

(a) Physical differences. Each individual is uniquely different with visible distinguishing features that include: height, weight, shape, colour of hair, eyes and skin, facial features, tone of voice, size of limbs and posture. Individual differences mean that it is possible to devise a specification of the requirements needed for a given job and in service industries it is particularly important to recruit individuals who possess an appropriate combination of qualities and attributes. For instance, it is desirable that a receptionist possesses an attractive, welcoming voice and that a porter has sufficient physical strength to undertake the work involved. The framework of legislation pertaining to employment also establishes requirements which employers must meet in respect of equality of opportunity (sex, ethnic origin and ratios of able-bodied and disabled employees). Equally, it is important for managers to be aware of the physical needs and requirements of customers and clients. For example, a typical hotel bed is longer now than it would have been a century ago, to reflect increases in the average height of the population.

Physical differences, accompanied by stereotyping can sometimes form the basis of a work culture. For example, the practice of grouping certain character traits under one gender type can lead to a 'macho' work culture where beliefs, values and attitudes reflect certain masculine traits such as aggression and competiveness:

"The Institute of Management published a survey reporting that the percentage of women managers has fallen from 10.2% in 1993 to 9.5% in 1994.(in 1983 it was 3.3%.)...women found it difficult to work in large firms that had a predominantly male culture and little flexibility for the needs of women." (*The Times,* 3 May 1994, p 7.)

Given the high proportion of women in working in the hospitality and tourism industries, it is vitally important for managers to provide working conditions that allow women to function effectively and achieve career advancement.

(b) Intelligence. A broad definition encompasses the abilities and skills that reflect the rational thinking and reasoning processes of the intellect or mind. Charles Handy (1) suggests that there are at least ten distinct types of intelligence. These are: (i) factual; (ii) logical or analytical; (iii) linguistic; (iv) mathematical; (v) musical; (vi) pattern-related (characterised by artists, programmers and entrepreneurs among others); (vii) practical; (viii) physical (athletic); (ix) psychic (intuition) and (x) interpersonal (the ability to work with others).

According to Handy, individuals progress through life accumulating portfolios of competence and intelligence. This suggests the need to be able to identify the type of intelligence required to undertake a particular job. As well as utilizing intelligence as productively as possible, managers are responsible for assisting and facilitating staff development. There are many forms of education, training and accreditation that can be harnessed for this purpose.

(c) Personality. Psychologists seek to define individual differences in relation to the concept of *personality.* Personality describes the features, characteristics and properties of the individual that provide both distinctiveness and stability (behavioural patterns, mannerisms, actions). It is debatable as to whether intelligence constitutes a dimension of personality or a separate and unique psychological mechanism. Further, some social scientists think that aspects of personality are inherited and/or determined by cultural, environmental and social factors. The main factors influencing personality developement are thought to be:

- *Genetic* - inherited traits such as physical structures and reflexes;

- *Environmental* - behaviour patterns acquired through interaction with others and with the environment encountered during socialization;

- *Cultural and social* - values, beliefs, customs, knowledge and skills learned as a result of being a member of a particular society or social group;

- *Situational* - unexpected or sudden events such as chance meetings, accidents, or deaths, that shape future behaviour and personality development.

Additionally, there are several popular 'dualistic' models of individual behaviour. They include:

Rational/emotional models. The rational model sees human beings as deliberative, serious and computational. The emotional model presents individuals as dominated by their emotions and internal conflict. This school of thought is directly related to Freud's theories of personality development.

Behaviouristic/humanistic models. The behavioural model describes individuals in terms of their behavioural patterns developed in response to environmental factors. The humanist model portrays individuals as creating and controlling their own destinies through the power of the human intellect.

Economic/self-actualizing models. The economic model views individuals as primarily motivated by the need to earn money to purchase goods and services. The self-actualizing model argues that individuals are mainly motivated by the desire to develop and grow to their full potential.

McGregor's theory x and y models. This approach can be used to explain managerial attitudes towards staff. *Theory x* portrays managers as mainly holding a negative view of the individual staff member. Here staff are considered to be inherently lazy, uncreative, and in need of constant supervision and encouragement. According to *theory y,* managers who take a more positive view by seeking to unlock the potential in people, can expect to see the benefits of their efforts realized in the form of a loyal, hard working and productive workforce.

Organizational structures, communication systems, and working practices will in part, reflect the individual manager's beliefs about human nature. For example, the manager who acts more in accordance with *theory x* might be more inclined towards structures that are hierarchal and bureaucratic. The manager who believes in the *theory y* approach will give greater autonomy and scope to staff and support the implementation of procedures that actively encourage participation. Likewise, managers in the behaviourist's mould will be concerned to identify and encourage behaviours that are considered to be essential to the success of the organization. Managers who are more sympathetic to the self-actualizing, emotional or humanistic models will be more inclined to recognize the holistic nature of a person's working life and seek to provide working conditions that are more flexible, such as job-share schemes.

These models are also relevant to the interpretation of customer needs and behaviour. If for example, managers believe that customers behave rationally and are motivated to maximize their satisfaction from a limited budget, they will focus on price competitiveness and discounting to encourage sales. , If on the other hand, the prevailing view is that customers routinely behave in an unpredictable, irrational way, managers might focus on creating qualitative differences so as to personalize an appeal to the emotions rather than a rational, economic purchase pattern.

Analyzing individual differences
(D: 2 pp 11-28)(2)
It is possible to assess personality differences in order to to identify individual potential using two approaches - *nomothetic* and *idiographic* analytic methods.

The *nomothetic* approach assumes personality is inherited and that dimensions of personality can be identified and measured by testing. Further, that a personality profile can be constructed across all of the dimensions measured. Eysenck for instance, identifies two major dimensions on which personality can vary: the *extraversion-introversion* or 'E' dimension, and the *neurotocism-stability* or 'N' dimension, and he has designed assessment tests for each (2 ch. 6 pp 101-109). There are problems with such assessments however, not least that questionnaires can never be subtle enough or sufficiently detailed to reveal the richness and complexity of an individual's thought patterns.

In contrast, the *idiographic* approach attempts to build a detailed picture of the individual using profiling and projection techniques. For example, the *thematic apperception test* seeks to encourage the individual to project his/her personality by means of writing a story (2 ch. 6 pp 116-118). The idiographic approach assumes that every individual possesses unique traits, that we are socially self-conscious, that we behave in accordance with the image that we have of ourselves and that we can change our personality through interaction with others.

Howard Gardner, a professor of education at Harvard University, identified and measured seven of the distinct types of intelligence listed earlier. Typically however, intelligence tests assess only one of forms, ususally factual intelligence or logical/analytical intelligence. If they are to be useful, intelligence tests must be reliable (give consistent results when repeated) and valid (measure what they claims to measure).

Implications for managers of hospitality and tourism organizations (D: 2 pp 11-28)
Understanding individual differences can prove useful as a basis for self-management, for the management of staff, and in understanding consumer behaviour. Managers need to be sensitive to individual differences throughout the process of recruiting, selecting, training and deploying staff. Recruitment information should be targeted at individuals with the necessary attributes for to fulfill the job description and specification. Selection methods should include a variety of techniques for assessing different aspects of the candidate's suitability for the job. Finally, during the training and deployment of staff, managers will need to create structures that are supportive and enable the employee to assimilate information in an appropriate way and at a suitable pace.

Argyris among others, has made the point that bureaucratic style organizations are unsuitable environments for an individual's personality to grow and mature.

"Argyris argued that the healthy personality develops naturally along a continuum from immaturity to maturity, but managerial practices in formal organizations can inhibit this natural maturation process. Lower level employees in particular are given minimal control over their work environment and are encouraged to be passive, dependent and subordinate...The challenge for management is to create work environments in which everyone has an opportunity to grow and mature as individuals." (2 ch. 16 p. 331)

In relation to consumer behaviour, a good example of how failure to fully understand individual and culturual differences can affect an organization has been provided by Euro-Disney. The Disney Corporation planned to replicate the American theme park experience in the suburbs of Paris (It opened in 1992). Disney made extensive quantitative projections of revenue, costs, likely daily attendance and occupancy rates, but in the event by early 1994 the park was heading for financial collapse (a rescue package was agreed in principle during March, 1994). A major omission seems to have been the inadequacy of market research relating to the predicted behavioural patterns of individuals likely to visit Euro-Disney. As as consequence, Disney did not appreciate how important alcohol is to the enjoyment of meals in Europe or that many visitors would only take a short-break at the park rather than the week-long vacation which is typical of Disney World in Florida. Nor had Disney fully appreciated how much Europeans would dislike queuing, or would be put off by the inclement weather. Some of the planning mistakes (such as the overbuilding of the hotel infrastructure) might have been avoided had Disney concentrated on psychographic (as distinct from demographic) market research. Psychographic research seeks to analyze how and why people behave in a certain way by gathering information about aspects of their personality (principally attitudes, interests, opinions, values and beliefs). In contrast, demographic research focuses more on objective dimensions of age, sex, income and life cycle.

CONCLUSION

Margaret Thatcher once commented that there was no such thing as society, there was only the individual.

In saying this, she must have been aware of the main changes taking place in Western lifestyles, the most significant of which perhaps is a growing desire for personal autonomy and independence. It is essential therefore, for managers of hospitality and tourism organizations to be aware of these trends as they impact on the attitudes, motivations and behaviours of customers and staff. Further, managers must be sensitive to individual differences and needs if they are to motivate staff and satisfy customers.

References:

1.   C. Handy. 'Style and Travel'. *Sunday Times,* 27 February, 1994, pp 18-19.

2.   D.A.Buchanan & A.A. Hucznski, *Organizational Behaviour*. Prentice-Hall, London, 1985.

3.   S. Willis. *A Primer For Daily Life*. Routledge, London, 1991.

4.   J. Lutz & C. Ryan. 'Hotels and the Business Woman.' *Tourism Management,* Butterworth-Heinemann, October, 1993 pp 349-356.

Review questions:

1.   'The historical theme park may be likened to a stage play where the audience joins the actors on stage' (3). Which personality traits do theme parks particularly appeal to, and what particular messages need to be conveyed by advertising media to attract customers with these traits?

2.   Consider the relationship between personality and self. To what extent is the true self suppressed beneath a false personality that is socially and culturally determined?

EXTENSION

Read: Chapter 23 and chapter 27 of *Supervisory Management: Principles and Practice..* (E: 23 pp 448-452; E: 27 pp 494 -498)

These chapters provide an outline of the most important aspects of the Sex Discrimination Acts of 1975-1986, the Race Relations Act of 1976 and a discussion of what constitutes lawful discrimination, sexual harassment and the implications for managers.

Extension questions:

1.   Evaluate the relevance of issues relating to 'gender' in the design and provision of services by hospitality and tourism organizations. For example: read (4) and assess the perception of hotel services by business women.

2.   Discuss the different methods a manager might adopt to reduce the incidence of: (a) sexual harassement and (b) discrimination against minorities.

3.   To what extent do hospitality and tourism organizations need to adopt a more feminine work culture?

Practical exercises:

Preparation: Try experiment 1, (C: 3 p.65) and using the framework provided in C: 3 (p. 62) design your own worksheet to faciliate the exercises set out below. The worksheet should address the following areas: (a) facial expression; (b) gaze and eye contact; (c) gesture; (d) body posture; (e) physical distance; (f) clothing and grooming. Self-assessment entries for the above points (a-f) should be made in relation to (i) skill strengths and (ii) skill weaknesses by drawing two columns on the worksheet.

1.   Analyze your general strengths and weaknesses in relation to each of the six areas (a-f). Now using a seperate worksheet ask a friend to undertake the same analysis (you should complete the same exercise for them). Discuss your findings and observations.

2.   To what extent do you think your body messages are affected by your cultural and sex-role conditioning?

3.   Where appropriate, set yourself goals for changing your body messages which aim to help you become a better communicator.

4.   Practice changing your body messages in real life to attain your goals.

2
PERCEPTIONS

INTRODUCTION

"We take a handful of sand from the endless landscape of awareness around us and call that handful of sand the world." From: R. M. Pirsig, *Zen and the Art of Motorcycle Maintenance.* Corgi Edition, New York, 1974, p. 75.

Every individual creates a personal picture of how they see the world around them. Individualistic pictures are based on samples of information upon which layers of meaning are imposed that provide a unique version of reality. In order to complete the picture, assumptions must be made about subjects, objects and situations and personal conclusions drawn. To illustrate, a subjective interpretation of the suitability of a particular hotel will include a projection of the experience of using the hotel and the type of service likely to be received. There are many implications for hospitality and tourism managers, who must seek to understand the general public's perceptions of the products and services on offer. Further, do for example, job seekers perceive good rewards and varied career opportunities? The concept of perception and its importance to managers, especially in service industries is the subject of this chapter.

In this chapter:
- The process of perception
  (A: 6 pp 77-78; B: 3 pp 33-39; C: 6 pp 155-158)
- Perceptual selectivity and perceptual organization (B: 3 pp 40-44) (1, ch. 3)
- Perceptual error and distortion
  (B: 3 pp 42-43; A: 6 pp 80-81)
- Ways of perceiving defensively
  (C: 10 p 240; B: 3 pp 42-43; A: 6 pp 91-99)
- How people can change their perceptions?
  (A: 6 pp 78-100; C: 6 pp 155-15; C: 10 pp 245-247; C: 11 pp 273-277)

REVIEW

The process of perception
(A: 6 pp 77-78; B: 3 pp 33-39; C: 6 pp 155-158)
Perception is the psychological process by which we become aware and make sense of the world around us.

It is thought that the brain invents an impression of the outside world from the fragmentary sampling of reality that the senses offer rather than relying solely on the senses to assimilate information. If for example, a customer walks into a self-service cafeteria and sees colourful fruit, smells fresh bread and hears soothing music he/she might conclude that it is a welcoming environment in which to eat. It is possible to liken these interactions to the creation of a hypothesis, tested by two further developments - *selection* and *organization.*

Perceptual selectivity and perceptual organization
(B: 3 pp 40-44)(1, ch. 3)
Perceptual selectivity involves filtering out unwanted information. It is only realistically possible to attend to small quantities of information at a time - information which is selected according to the given situation, circumstances and likely events. The mass of data conveyed to the brain every second via the five senses: hearing, sight, smell, taste and touch is therefore filtered to avoid overload. Further, prior experience and personal preferences generally determine the way in which information is interpreted. For example, the personnel director of a hotel chain may honestly feel that he or she is choosing the best person for the job, but unconscious influences such as age, sex, or race preferences may bias an objective assessment of whether a particular candidate has the right blend of qualities, skills and experiences.

Perceptual organization is the mechanism by which individuals make sense of selected information by ordering, systemizing, patterning and imposing meaning. Wherever possible, new stimuli are interpreted in relation to prior knowledge and experience. Stimuli are organized in three ways. First, they are visualized in relation to a relevant background, not in isolation. The restaurant supervisor for example, attempting to assess the competence of staff in action, will see individual staff against a background of chairs, tables, music lighting and the operational characteristics and features of the restaurant. Second, stimuli are grouped together and classified according to whether they are close to each other (the proximity principle) or similar in appearance to each other (the similarity principle). For example, a contract caterer wishing to maximize sales, generally displays related food items such as ice cold cans, sandwiches and chocolate. The products are perceived as snack meal components essential to the enjoyment of a particular meal type. Consequently it is more likely that all three items will be purchased. Third, the human brain seeks to fill incomplete gaps and ambiguous patterns of stimuli so as to make them more meaningful. This is called the closure principle.

Managers needs to be aware of this when communicating information to staff. Communication that are badly worded or contain incomplete information may mean that a different message is conveyed to that intended.

The selection and organization process while helping to avoid information overload can result in the neglect of other important stimuli. For instance, the person who formulates the hypothesis that the fish and chip restaurant is clean and hygienic because of the clean white marble effect flooring, may be so taken in by this impression that he or she fails to observe other less pleasing sights. In general, stimuli that are large, in motion, intense, novel, familiar, or contrasting are likely to have the biggest initial impact. Stimuli that are small, stationary, less intense or that blend with their background are less memorable. If for instance customers at a holiday camp or leisure complex experience a problem, they are usually drawn to the person in uniform who is percieved to trustworthy and most likely to be helpful.

The selection and organization of material is related to the individual's perceptual world or set. In turn, the set is influenced by personally meaningful factors like prior experience, motives, needs, psychological characteristics and behaviour as well as the physical, social and cultural environment. This background knowledge and experience can contribute to inaccuracies and errors during the selection and organization of new stimuli. A series of inaccurate judgements and evaluations are likely to have a cumulative effect and create a form of perceptual distortion. If for example, an interviewer's perception of a candidate is partially inaccurate, it may mean that a suitable person for a particular job is rejected.

Perceptual error and distortion
(A: 6 pp 80-81; A: 6 pp 91-99; B: 3 pp 42-43; C: 10 p 240)
Sources of perceptual error most commonly occur in one or more of the following ways: (a) insufficient information or (b) irrelevant information is received; (c) information is screened in such a way that the person only sees what he or she wants to see; (d) prior information affects a person's perception of new information; (e) personal preferences affect the way in which others are perceived or (f) stereotypical information is accepted without re-examination.

Sources of perceptual error that can contribute to a poor self-image or negative view of other people include:

- *Negativity* - over emphasizing negative aspects of self or others.

- *Personalizing* - perceiving self as the centre of attention.
- *Overgeneralizing* - drawing a general conclusion from a specific observation.
- *Black and white thinking* - in either/or terms.
- *Misattributing* - inaccurately diagnosing the cause of certain behaviours relating to actions by self or others.

In practice these and other perceptual errors often overlap and/or occur in clusters so they are difficult to control.

Defensiveness (or the defence mechanism) is the means by which an individual manipulates incoming information so as to reduce levels of personal anxiety. The objective is to maintain consistency of self-image both internally and externally as projected to others. The operation of a defence mechanism can distance a person from reality and can contribute to serious relationship problems. One of the most important aspects of the defence mechanism is *projection*. This is the tendency to ascribe personal feelings and attributes to others in order to avoid facing up to unpleasant home truths. For example, a trainer is holding a workshop on presentation skills for hospitality and tourism managers. She has had a sleepless night following a major row with her partner and is feeling uptight and tired. The last thing she feels like doing is taking a class. Fifteen minutes into the workshop one class member yawns and another starts to chat. The trainer gets annoyed and snaps 'I wish to goodness you wouldn't sit there yawning and chatting. If you're not interested why bother turning up?' The trainer thus projects her own partially repressed feelings to the students. In fact it is she who is tired and wishing she hadn't turned up.

The converse of projection is *introjection* which occurs when a person adopts characteristics that really belong to someone else. A person might feel afraid for example, because fear is sensed in someone else. Alternatively an individual may take on the characteristics and copy the behaviour of a well liked manager.

Other facets of the defence mechanism include *avoidance* (avoiding anything that causes anxiety or discomfort); *defensive lying* (making-up stories to attach blame to someone else) and *distortion* (when incoming information is processed in such a way as to maintain a particular view of self). The ultimate defence mechanism action is *denial* where information which is threatening or frightening is totally blocked-off from the person's conscious awareness.

Other important features of human perceptual processes that can cause error or distortion are stereotyping and the halo effect.

Stereotyping is the tendency to make simplistic judgements and form generalizations about people or objects on the basis of limited knowledge and experience. Stereotyping occurs when an individual attributes particular attitudes and behaviours to another person as a consequence of that person's membership of a class, group or category and as a result of a widely held view that the group or category has certain definitive characteristics. Stereotyping simplifies the individual's interpersonal world. Instead of relating to people on the basis of their individuality, we relate to them as a representative of a class, group, or category. For example, consider advertising that is primarily targeted at women. As Sarah Newman, a planner with the advertising agency Ogilvy and Mather states: "*an awful lot of time and effort is put into understanding a young male audience...their moods,emotions and attitudes were analyzed in detail and were reflected in commercials for cars and lager. Women,on the other hand, have been stereotyped as housewives, mothers, sex objects or career women. And who is doing most of the nation's shopping? Yes, women!*". (2)

Why does such stereotyping of women occur in commercials? Is it because the design and control of commercials is mainly undertaken by men who hold stereotypical views of women? This issue of the stereotyping of women in advertising is particularly relevant to the tourism industry. Holiday brochure design is becoming increasingly geared towards those who choose and book - in short towards women: "*Photographs...aim to develop perceptions of the 'nuclear' family, the girl next door image, stylish hotel rooms and tempting shops. Women are pictured sipping drinks on a terrace or lounging by a pool, but you are never likely to see one cooking, even in a villa.*" (3)

The halo effect refers to an individual's initial impression of another person, which then forms the basis for judgements about more specific traits, attitudes and behaviours. For example, a particularly outstanding report completed just prior to a performance evaluation may result in a highly positive appraisal for the entire preceding period. The halo effect operates in both *negative* and *positive* directions. For example, an interviewer may dislike a certain regional accent. This may negatively distort his judgement of an applicant who speaks with this particular accent.

The same interviewer might on the other hand, associate formal clothes with trust and confidence and be more favourably disposed towards someone who dresses that way for an interview. To reduce the halo effect, managers need to be aware that appearances can be deceptive and other forms of information may be required in order to evaluate specific behaviours.

How people can change their perceptions?
(A: 6 pp 78-100; C: 6 pp 155-159; C: 10 pp 245-247; C: 11 pp 273-277)
There are a number of practical steps that can help to improve self-perceptions and overcome sources of perceptual bias, distortion and error. These are: (i) evaluate personal feelings and perceptions; (ii) seek to develop more positive perceptions; (iii) let go of defensiveness and (iv) seek to perceive self and others more positively.

(i) Evaluate personal feelings and perceptions.
A starting point is to develop a greater awareness of self-defeating perceptions and perceptual errors that can culminate in negative feelings. This can be done by carefully monitoring self-talk and by making a note of negative feelings as and when they occur. The next step is to analyze how information is filtered, selected and organized by reflecting and acting on a number of key questions: (a) is each perception based on fact or inference? (b) does the perception contain error or distortion? (c) is there any other information available to increase the accuracy of the perception?

(ii) Seek to develop more positive perceptions.
A person needs to develop self-valuing, supportive and confidence-building perceptions by: (a) becoming aware of negative self-labels; (b) consciously selecting more positive perceptions and (c) being prepared to accept and 'own' positive self-perceptions.

(iii) Let go of defensiveness.
Accept that everyone has their defences. Self-awareness can then be developed by identifying the nature and type of defence mechanism used and the situations in which each is brought into play. Alternative ways of reacting can then be considered, tried and evaluated.

(iv) Seek to perceive self and others more positively.
This involves: (a) collecting new information; (b) trying to understand the causes of other peoples' behaviour; (c) taking responsibility for one's own behaviour; (d) experimenting with new perceptions of other people and (e) improving specific relationship skills.

CONCLUSION

"We cannot with any certainty imagine ourselves inside another's consciousness. All we can be sure of is our own, which means, paradoxically that we are certain only of what we cannot describe or measure." (4)

Perceptual distortion is most likely to occur when making 'snap' judgements about other people. Although first impressions can hasten decision-making in the short-term thereby reducing time and costs; in the longer term it may well lead to a mis-allocation of resources, lower productivity and dissatisfaction. It is therefore vitally important for hospitality and tourism managers to be aware of the way in which they perceive information. The attitudes and behaviours that result from perceptual errors can cause serious organizational problems and so an understanding of the perceptual process is essential to the management of self and others.

References:

1.   D.A.Buchanan & A.A. Huczynski. *Organizational Behaviour.* Prentice Hall, London, 1985.

2.   G.Thomas. 'Brochures Go for Mother Appeal' *The Times,* 2 December, 1993.

3.   L.Brinkworth. 'Housewives and Nauseam' Style and Travel, *Sunday Times,* 28 November, 1993.

4.   J.Carey. 'Sugared Almonds and Weeping Policemen.' Books section, *Sunday Times,* 3 April, 1994.

Review questions:

1.   Consider how differences in perceptions can cause problems for managers of: (a) a restaurant; (b) a hotel and (c) an airline operator.

2.   One of the main difficulties facing interviewers is the pheonomenon of perceptual distortion. Discuss.

3.   Consider the relevance of understanding the process of perception to the design of theme parks.

EXTENSION

Read: Chapter 11 of *People and the Hotel and Catering Industry.* (D: 11 pp 176-189)

This chapter considers the nature of the 'hospitality product' in relation to consumer behaviour. The process of perception is an important influence on the design and provision of the product, on the decision to purchase, on the feelings associated with its use and on its subsequent evaluation.

Extension questions:

1.   Examine the different methods used by hospitality and tourism organizations to shift perceptions of quality held by customers so as to maintain and increase their profitability.

2.   Examine the relationships between perception and motivation. Consider the implications of this relationship for the design of an advertising campaign aimed at the short-break tourist market.

3.   One of the problems faced by the British Tourist Authority (BTA) in marketing the U.K. to the Japanese is apparently that Japanese women perceive the British male as macho, aggressive and militaristic. How might such perceptions have arisen and how might the BTA change these perceptions?

Practical exercises:

1.   Assess your own perceptions by working through 'Thinksheet 20' (A: 6 pp 79-80).

2.   After completing the practical exercise (1) decide on a day when you will take a complete break from your normal routine. For example, dress in a different way, add some accessory you don't normally wear, alter your hairstyle, act differently, do something you don't normally do or go somewhere you don't normally go. Keep a record of your perceptions during the day using Thinksheet 20. Compare the two days and make a note of what you have learned about your own perceptions.

3.   Visit a supermarket and make a note of all the methods used to influence consumer perceptions of quality. Consider how such methods might be applied to a hotel or restaurant operation.

3

RELATIONSHIPS

INTRODUCTION

"With love comes heartache. This is a fact of life and not as negative as it seems at first. If you don't care deeply for someone disagreements and problems will only be a passing annoyance. The more someone matters to you, the more you will mind when things between you go wrong." S. Litvinoff, 'The Relate Guide to Better Relationships'. Ebury Press, London 1991, p 9.

The psychoanalyst R.D. Lang once commented that if we were totally on our own in the world we would quickly go insane. He was making the point that though we are each in essence, isolated and potentially lonely, we strive to break out of our isolation by making contact with other people. Moreover, we seek to affirm our existence (confirming and reinforcing who and what we are) by making contact and relating to others. A relationship then is basically a point of reference or connection. Good connections are one of the main ingredients of success in all walks of life. Success for hospitality and tourism organizations depends on good relationships between employers, management, the workforce, suppliers, contractors, external agents (such as local government) and customers. Managers need to understand the basis of good relationships and use the insights gained to connect and develop the relationships required to succeed, both in human and financial terms. This chapter examines the scope of relationships and the implications for maintaining them effectively.

In this chapter:
- Relationships (C: 1 pp 1-20)
- The basis of a good relationship
  (C: 1 pp 1-20; C: 2 pp 21-55; A: 11 pp 198-201)
- Relationships and the hospitality and tourism manager (D: 6 pp 82-90)
- Relationship skills (C: 3 pp 56-86; A: 1 pp 1-12; A: 6 pp 95-100; A: 11 pp 198-201)

REVIEW

Relationships
(C: 1 pp 1-20)
Individuals endeavour to form the relationships necessary to satisfy physiological, emotional and intellectual needs.

Relationships in economic, social, political and cultural environments each have different goals. These include:

- *economic environment* - through the acts of production and consumption to satisfy the need to survive, compete, achieve, gain security and acquire status and wealth.

- *social environment* - through friendships, peer groups, shared interests and common purposes to satisfy the individual's need for intimacy, bonding, pleasure, loyalty, trust, emotional and sexual satisfaction.

- *political environment* - through networking, lobbying and voting to satisfy the individual's need for conflict resolution, representation, status, freedom and power.

- *cultural environment* - via activities such as religion, art, drama and music which seek to satisfy the individual's need for self-expression, social acceptance and spiritual harmony.

Managers need to develop and take account of relationships in each of these environmental domains. Key economic and political relationships include:

- *economic* - relationships with and between shareholders, customers, the workforce and suppliers.

- *political* - relationships with locally elected representatives, government officials and managers of relevant public bodies (for example, Tourist Boards).

By its very nature the hospitality/tourism organization seeks to provide and promote activities that encourage social relationships and which reflect popular culture.

The basis of a good relationship
(C: 1 pp 1-20; C: 2 pp 21-55; A: 11 pp 198-201)
Popular culture provides an idyllic image of romantic love, passion, erotocism and freedom - we meet the right person and sail off to our island of dreams. Romantic love may intially seem effortless because the initial joy is in *being loved,* rather than on being loving.

In reality, good relationships don't just happen, they are normally the result of commitment and joint effort. Perfect relationships are as much an illusion as perfect love but the basis of a 'quality relationship' is nonetheless a loving, selfless attitude of mind.

Love is defined by Nelson-Jones as making choices that affirm both yourself and others in your relationships. A loving relationship therefore involves both parties, each enhancing the other through the giving, receiving and sharing of affection, while trying to confront and satisfactorily manage each others' vulnerabilities and anxieties. These principles can be applied to all relationships, both personal and in business situations.

A second important requirement for a quality relationship is mutual need satisfaction and with it the concept of exchange. This, while essential to a personal relationship, is also particularly relevant to relationships of an economic nature. The consumer exchanges money for the utility provided by the good or service. An occasional source of discontent in personal relationships is the mistaken belief that one individual can somehow fully satisfy the needs of another. Relationships are subtle mixtures of differences and similarities between the individuals concerned. Perfect matches are rare, and more probably some of the differences and similarities have to be satisfied by other relationships.

A third ingredient of a quality relationship is negotiation and compromise in support of conflict resolution. All relationships experience conflict in some form and in this sense exhibit a political dimension (the struggle for power and control). Work environments for example, are often characterized by destructive conflicts which can cause stress and lower output. Conflict however can lead to positive results, such as creative solutions to problems.

A fourth dimension is communication - the ability to convey one's meaning to others. Effective communication requires an ability to identify and disclose self needs, together with an ability to listen and respond helpfully to the need disclosure of others.

Relationships and the hospitality and tourism manager (D: 6 pp 82-90)

The key interpersonal relationships that affect the daily work and routine of managers are: (a) personal effectiveness and relationships with: (b) senior management; (c) customers; (d) the workforce; (e) other managers; (f) suppliers and external agents; (g) providers of finance and professional services and (h) the media. If one or more of these relationships is unsatisfactory, conflict and poor communication may arise.

(a) Personal effectiveness.
This is mainly concerned with the extent to which the individual manager can minimize the impact of stress on his/her performance and maximize personal effectiveness. Failure to do this can lead to a sub-standard performance and possibly de-motivate junior staff, with potentially damaging consequences for relationships with customers.

(b) Relationships with senior management.
The manager needs to be aware of senior management's objectives, pressures and constraints. Information must be channelled downwards so that managers can facilitate the day-to-day running of the business and upwards from managers to senior management so as to support strategic planning, financial control and resource management.

(c) Relationships with customers.
The manager's role includes customer support and in some circumstances it is appropriate to communicate directly with customers so as to enhance their experience of the product or service. For example, the hotel manager asking the guests how they are enjoying their stay, or the restaurant manager wishing the diners 'bon appetite'. Failure to develop and maintain an effective relationship with the customer may ultimately lead to loss of business.

(d) Relationships with the workforce.
Managers need to 'walk and talk' (mix with staff, listen to their problems, take note of their views, and disseminate relevant information); manage change and conflict; establish effective working groups with a suitable mix of skills and personality types and respond to problems generated by particular relationships. Failure to harmonize relationships between employees can be costly. In the short term it can mean reduced productivity through friction, stress, absenteeism or strikes. In the longer term, if working relationships continue to deteriorate, it can have an adverse affect on the organization's reputation as an employer.

(e) Relationships with other managers.
In large organizations it is essential that managers work harmoniously with each other and with supervisors and staff. Cooperation is needed to collate information to coordinate activities and to complete other tasks necessary to the achievement of organizational goals. The effectiveness of working relationships will, to some extent be hindered by competitive rivalry between managers and/or their departments and the prevailing style of organizational politics.

Inevitably, working relationships are influenced by personal objectives like gaining advancement or a bigger share of organizational resources and so a continual effort is needed to reinforce a teamwork approach.

In smaller organizations, it is sensible for managers to meet with other managers working in similar sized organizations to share and discuss problems and to stimulate new ideas.

(f) Relationships with suppliers and external agents.
Managers need to cultivate harmonious relationships with suppliers so as to ensure the prompt delivery of goods and services at the right time and place and to the correct specification. If these requirements are not met, the nature of the relationship with a supplier should enable problems to be resolved quickly and amicably. Equally, relationships with other external agents, such as local government, must be established and maintained to ensure the best possible relations with the community. This is an especially important channel of communication and there are many informal sources of information which can provide useful forms of intelligence relating to hospitality and tourism business.

(g) Relationships with providers of finance and professional services.
Managers need to maintain good working relationships with the organization's bank, insurance company, and accountant among others. For example, a manager with innovative ideas may find it difficult to obtain the necessary finances to put them into practice if the organization has neglected to build up relations with its bank and other appropriate financial institutions.

(h) Relationships with the media.
Bad publicity can destroy a business, while good publicity can help it grow. A good relationship with the press and local radio and television can raise the profile of the organization in the public's mind.

Relationship skills (C: 3 pp 56-86; A: 1 pp 1-12; A: 6 pp 95-100; A: 11 pp 198-201)
The fundamental relationship skills that managers need to develop and the specific behaviours associated with each skill are:

Self-awareness. In order to relate well to other people, first you have to relate effectively to yourself. One of the main aims of this book is to raise levels of self-awareness in this regard.

Listening. The ability to empathize with other people is an important managerial skill. Effective listening equates with an ability to understand the thoughts of the speaker and thereby interpret the communication from his or her point of view.

Self-disclosure. There are five ways of disclosing thoughts and feelings to others: body messages; touch messages (physical contact); voice messages (how you talk); verbal messages (what you say) and action messages (what you do).

Using oral persuasion. Oral persuasion can be defined as the conscious, verbal manipulation of symbols (words) to induce others to take action (1). Persuasion (rather than coercion) is vitally important in building and sustaining relationships with others.

Providing feedback. Performance feedback can in its most positive form, constitute encouragement and recognition. This is an effective way of motivating people to achieve further performance improvements.

Goal setting. Employees, like managers need a clear sense of direction and purpose that can be fulfilled by a clearly defined role, responsibilities and personal goals or targets for their work.

Resolving conflicts. To manage conflict effectively, managers need to be aware of themselves, (strengths and weaknesses) and an ability to assess the causes, consequences and potential solutions to conflict with others. This includes the ability to interpret the situation or event(s) causing the conflict and an awareness of the options for resolving it. Resolving conflict requires skill in goal setting, listening, feedback, oral persuasion, anger management, assertion, and problem-solving.

Coping with organizational politics. Politically motivated action relates to the steps taken to influence, or attempt to influence, the organizational decision-making processes. To succeed, it is necessary to: (a) frame arguments in relation to organizational goals; (b) develop an appropriate image; (c) gain access to organizational resources; (d) ensure that key decision-makers perceive the value of the arguments put forward; (e) maintain a visible organizational profile; (f) win friends and allies; (g) avoid involvement in project 'failures' and (h) remain loyal to superiors, close colleagues and allies.

Other relationship skills. There are other specialist skills that managers can and should seek to develop in order to build and sustain good working relationships with others. These include: developing and leading teams; delegating and skills relating to recruitment, selection, appraisal and taking disciplinary action.

CONCLUSION

What differentiates a successful manager from an unsuccessful one? Studies consistently show that good relationship skills are critical to managerial success (1). This is increasingly the case in hospitality and tourism as managerial work at all levels and in every functional specialism attains full professional status. Relationships play a key role in the smooth functioning of organizations and the array of skills needed to cope successfully with the demands of a service business provide a career-long challenge for all who aspire to a senior management position.

Reference:

1.   S.P. Robbins, *Training in Interpersonal Skills*. Prentice-Hall, London, 1989.

Review questions:

1.   What are the most important behaviours needed to ensure good relationships between staff and (a) hotel guests; (b) restaurant diners and (c) pub customers?

2.   How might a manager promote good working relationships between (a) younger and older staff and (b) staff of different ethnic backgrounds?

3.   How might a manager encourage customers to relate to the products and services provided by (a) a fast food outlet; (b) a leisure complex and (c) a tour operator so as to stimulate repeat purchases?

EXTENSION

Read: Chapters 2, 3 and 5 of *Human Relationship Skills* (C: 2, 3:& 5 pp 56- 141)

In these chapters, Nelson-Jones descibes how to improve relationships with others. In particular, how to listen effectively and how to respond in the most helpful way. Consider then the following situation:

Kelly King is a shift manager at a fast food restaurant. She supervises twenty staff including Sue Thomas. Sue is a twenty-two year old graduate and has just completed a three month probationary period. Kelly is required to undertake Sue's performance review. Kelly wants to use the opportunity to tell Sue that while her job performance has in general been satisfactory, two things concern her.

First, Sue has long hair and is required by health regulations to wear a hair net, but she regularly fails to do this. Second, Sue has been dating Paul another employee in the restaurant. Kelly is concerned that they are often touching each other while working behind the counter. Kelly decides to extend the probation by one month and give Sue a small pay increase. Sue who would have left if she hadn't formed a relationship with Paul, doesn't think much of Kelly as a manager, but expects to be made permanent and awarded a signficant pay increase.

Extension questions:

1.   Consider the range of messages (body, touch, voice, verbal, action) that (a) Kelly might direct at Sue and (b) Sue might use during the course of the review with Kelly. Appraise the relative importance and role of the non-verbal messages given out by each person during the performance review.

2.   Imagine yourself in Sue's role. How would you prepare for the performance review with Kelly and what would you say?

3.   What are the most important relationship skills for a manager of a fast food restaurant to possess?

4.   What are the most important relationship skills that fast food restaurant staff should demonstrate in respect of customers?

Practical exercises:

Task: Complete exercises 1 to 9 in C: 3.

1.   Imagine that you have a good friend who has a mannerism (speech, body movement, style of dress, or the like) that you think is inappropriate and detracts from the overall impression that he or she makes. Explain how you would help your friend to appreciate this, and change the mannerism. How would you cope with your friend's initial reactions (anger, hurt feelings, sullen silence etc.)?

2.   Think of three tasks that a friend did well recently. Did you praise the person at the time? If not, why? The next time the friend does something well, give him or her some positive feedback. Appraise the way in which the person reacts, both in terms of verbal and non-verbal behaviour.

4
LISTENING

INTRODUCTION

"A long time ago in China there were two friends, one who played the harp skilfully and one who listened skilfully. When the player played about water, the listener would exclaim: "Here is the running stream". When the listener fell sick and died the player cut the strings of his harp and never played again." (A traditional Zen story) P.Baguley, *Effective Communications For Modern Business.* McGraw-Hill, England, 1994.

Being an effective communicator involves appreciating the processes of gathering and transmitting information and feelings from one individual to another. An essential part of this process is the feedback which the receiver gives. The receiver, therefore, needs to develop the skill of listening; understanding and decoding the verbal and body messages of the transmitter.

For managers in the hospitality and tourism industries listening to others is an important part of their work. For example, staff have problems which they need to discuss and customers require information and advice. It is important to realise that whilst individuals may be born with the capacity to hear, this does not automatically mean that they are good listeners. The purpose of this chapter is to identify the techniques of effective listening and to review the barriers that can prevent respect and acceptance of others. The importance of non-verbal communication is examined as is the skill of encouraging others to discuss their feelings.

In this chapter:
- The importance of effective listening (C: 4 p 88)
- Techniques of effective listening (D: 4 p 74)
- Understanding another's viewpoint (C: 4 pp 90-93)
- Respecting and accepting others (C: 4 pp 94-100; D: 4 p 77)
- Positive non-verbal communication (C: 4 pp 100-106)
- Voice messages (C: 4 pp 106-108)
- Encouraging others to talk (C: 4 pp 108-110)

REVIEW

The importance of effective listening (C: 4 p 88)
Listening to what others have to say is a positive act which is a rewarding experience for the individual who is in the role of transmitter. For young people the quality of listening of the adults that are close to them is an essential part of their psychological development. When individuals are listened to they feel more confident about expressing their feelings and are less likely to feel insecure, angry or aggressive.

Being an effective listener creates an atmosphere where others feel safe and able to be natural. In essence they are not defensive and as a result they feel they can be 'open' about their worries and concerns. Listening to others also provides the opportunity for feedback and personal development.

Exchanging inner secrets is a process which is based on a willingness to listen and to trust each other. Rewarding listening also builds trust and stability in relationships by assisting individuals to prevent and manage problems. The more people are able to express what they really think and feel the less likely it is that misunderstandings will occur. Where problems do develop, if people listen to each other the difficulties will usually be resolved.

It is important to remember that differences exist between the backgrounds and experiences of people. There is a danger that an individual may have 'tunnel vision' and not understand the circumstances of others. By listening carefully to what people say an understanding can be gained and bridges can be built.

Techniques of effective listening (D: 4 p 74)
The first technique for being a good listener involves demonstrating an open approach to the communicator and this means:

- Concentrating on what is being transmitted;
- Listening actively;
- Questioning any misunderstandings;
- Asking for clarification and repetition where necessary;
- Illustrating through non-verbal communication that the message is being received and understood.

Being a good listener is hard work and is a skill which is acquired with practise. Concentrating on what another person says involves giving them complete attention and asking questions at appropriate stages.

For example a purchasing manager for a contract catering company listening to presentations from food suppliers will need to remember all the key details concerning prices, discounts, quality standards and delivery systems. Before a contract is agreed with a supplier the purchasing manager will need to clarify any areas of doubt and possibly ask for statements to be repeated e.g. the amount of notice required for extra goods to be delivered.

The second technique confirms that the message has been understood correctly and this is achieved by:

- Paraphrasing and repeating the message;
- Giving feedback on the feelings which have been transmitted;
- Negotiating the interpretation of the message.

There are occasions when it is very important to check the details of what has been said. For example an individual who is receiving instructions on how to operate a piece of equipment will need to ensure that they have understood the process correctly. Throughout the listening process it is also important to be aware of the non-verbal signals and to avoid any barriers to understanding.

Understanding another's viewpoint
(C: 4 pp 90-93)
In order to fully understand the views of another person it is necessary to appreciate the differences which exist. By demonstrating an accurate perception of another's viewpoint the individual is responding as if they are in their position i.e. 'in their shoes'. This is referred to as an internal viewpoint. For example a hospitality or tourism manager conducting an appraisal interview with a member of staff may express the following internal viewpoint: 'you feel that you have the necessary skills and experience to move into a supervisory position'. Developing such an internal viewpoint requires careful listening and the interpretation of messages by understanding voice and body signals. In contrast an external viewpoint is not based on understanding the situation of the other person. An external viewpoint could be: 'I am interested in what you are doing in your current job, not what you think you could be doing'.

Respecting and accepting others
(C: 4 pp 94 -100; D: 4 p 77)
Whilst the distinction between listening from an internal and external viewpoint is relatively easy to understand, putting it into practice is more difficult. The first step involves an individual respecting and accepting themselves. This affects the level of acceptance and respect, and as a result quality of listening, which an individual can give to another.

It is important to appreciate that everyone has their own thoughts and feelings which need to be respected. A secure individual will not build barriers and filters or completely block an incoming message. Barriers to an accepting attitude include:

- *Strong feelings*. Particularly strong positive or negative feelings can affect the ability to listen carefully to what others are saying.

- *Trigger words and phrases*. These words and phrases are spoken in a way which can be interpreted as 'put downs' or alternatively, flattery. For example 'you should really follow my advice' or 'you always achieve good results'. In essence words and phrases which are emotionally charged can interfere with the listening process.

- *Unfinished business*. Previous experiences such as a disagreement with an individual may result in less patience being given to listening to the next person they come into contact with.

- *Anxiety-evoking topics*. For a variety of reasons there are some topics which individuals prefer not to discuss. If these topics are raised it can cause feelings of anxiety.

- *Prejudice*. It may be difficult to relate to others due to prejudice. The individual differences will be related to age, culture, race etc.

- *Anxiety-evoking people*. Sometimes individuals or groups can lead to feelings of anxiety and this causes a barrier to effective listening. Figures in authority such as parents may fall into this category.

- *Anxiety-evoking situations*. Certain situations are always stressful. For example giving a presentation to a potential client interested in booking a conference or explaining to a member of staff why they need to improve their standard of work. The tension of such situations can affect the ability to hear what is being said.

- *Bringing the past into the present*. Past experiences and reactions to them can be brought forward to present situations. The past may evoke positive or negative feelings.

- *Conflict with self picture*. It may be difficult for an individual to adopt an accepting attitude when others have a different picture of them.

- *Physical barriers.* Due to tiredness, illness, or noise it may be difficult to listen effectively to what others have to say.

Other reasons why the receiver may not listen to others include the insecurity which arises from a lack of understanding about the reasons for the communication. For example an individual who has been called to a meeting with his supervisor to discuss a new rota system may not listen carefully to what is being said because he does not understand that the company is having to cut costs. There may also be a lack of trust in the sender which leads to a reluctance to ask questions. The problem could arise because too much information has overloaded the receiver or alternatively the sender has not motivated the receiver to listen.

Positive non-verbal communication
(C: 4 pp 100-106)
Attention to what is being said by another person can be demonstrated in the form of body messages (1). These include:

- *Physical availability.* The pace of life can mean that people have little time to dedicate to listening to others. For example a busy manager may not have enough time to speak to all his or her staff and this in effect means that they have withdrawn their interest and attention. A manager who sets aside time regularly for discussions with staff is demonstrating a positive availability message.

- *Body posture.* A relaxed body posture promotes the message that the individual concerned is emotionally accessible.

- *Personal space.* Individuals may feel that their personal space is being invaded if the communicator leans too far forward. In the same way leaning back too far can give an impression of 'distancing' oneself from the situation.

- *Gestures.* The most common gesture when listening to others is to head nod. This shows that the listener is attentive. Other gestures include arms and hands which can be used to demonstrate responsiveness to a speaker. Negative gestures include clenched hands and crossed arms.

- *Eye gaze and contact.* The acceptable level of eye contact is dependent on factors such as cultural rules and the level of anxiety. The eyes can be used to signal tension or boredom. Gaze can give cues about when to stop listening and start responding.

- *Facial expressions.* A smile is a very positive way of conveying interest when listening to others. For staff involved with guests in a hotel, facial expressions can help to make people feel welcome.

- *Physical distance and height.* Moving too quickly into another's personal space may make them feel ill at ease. Standing whilst the other person is sitting can create a tense situation.

- *Touch.* One way of showing concern for another individual is to touch them. In so doing, it must be made clear by means of verbal communication and/or facial expression that this is intended solely as a gesture of support.

The more that body, voice and verbal messages are in harmony the more likely an individual will be perceived as a rewarding listener. For instance a manager who smiles whilst talking to staff but also keeps looking at their watch may send conflicting messages of interest and impatience. It is very important that individuals appreciate the negative effects that poor listener body messages can result in. In a study by Haase and Tepper (2) it was found that even good verbal understanding messages could be reduced to poor ones when there was no eye contact. Sending good body messages is an essential part of being a rewarding listener.

Voice messages (C: 4 pp 106-108)
Speakers need to feel that individuals are responsive to their feelings. This can be achieved by sending voice messages which do not affect the meaning and emphasis. The following should be taken into consideration:

- *Volume.* The level should be easy to listen to.
- *Pace.* Avoid talking too fast and interrupting.
- *Emphasis.* The voice should express feelings accurately.
- *Tone.* A harsh tone can sound threatening.
- *Enunciation.* Responses should be made clearly.
- *Accent.* Heavy accents can be difficult to understand.
- *Pauses.* Good use of silences and pauses can give speakers time to think before talking.

Encouraging others to talk (C: 4 pp 108-110)
There are occasions when individuals need to be encouraged to discuss their feelings. The process involves being sensitive to others and their reactions. For example a manager dealing with a member of staff who has personal problems may find they are reluctant to speak to them about their difficulties.

It is important to respect the wishes of the person concerned but where appropriate, pose questions which allow the individual to share their internal viewpoint. It is also important to avoid negative outcomes such as being classed as an interrogator. Openers, small rewards and open-ended questions each make it easier for a speaker to talk. An example of an opener is: 'I would like to hear your viewpoint.' Using openers requires sensitivity to the other's reactions. Small rewards are expressions of interest which encourage the speaker. An example is: 'please continue'. Open questions allow speakers to share their internal viewpoint. An example is: 'How do you feel about promoting Daniel?' All three of these techniques are designed to help others communicate what they think and feel.

CONCLUSION

Listening is one of the most effective ways of complimenting another individual and yet few people have fully developed the skill. There are a range of techniques which can be used to improve the effectiveness of the listening process such as concentrating on what is being transmitted. Fully appreciating that others have different viewpoints is an important step to being a good listener as is responding and accepting others.

There are a number of barriers to an accepting attitude such as strong feelings and prejudice. Non-verbal communication has a significant part to play in the listening process as does the tone and volume of the voice. Finally there are techniques which can be used to encourage others to discuss their feelings.

References:

1.	A.E.Ivey. *Microcounselling: Innovations in Interviewing Training.* Springfield, IL: Charles C. Thomas, 1971.
2.	R.F.Haase & D.Tepper. 'Nonverbal Components of Empathic Communication', *Journal of Counselling Psychology,* 19, 417-424, 1972.

Review questions:

1.	Discuss the extent to which hospitality or tourism managers should aim to understand the viewpoints of their staff.

2.	From your experience, describe a situation where you did not listen effectively. Discuss the barriers which caused the problem.

3.	Discuss the importance of non-verbal communication for staff in the hospitality and tourism industries.

EXTENSION

Read: Chapter 2 of *Personal Effectiveness* (F: 2 pp 17-37).

This chapter addresses the development of interpersonal skills. The aim is to assist individuals in the establishment of working relationships and self development. The introduction reviews the nature of interpersonal communication and distinguishes between verbal and non-verbal components. Gender and cultural differences are explored next along with first impressions. The chapter then moves on to examine the factors which facilitate effective communication and focuses on motivation and delegation as part of the process. The final part of the chapter concentrates on the development of assertiveness.

Extension questions:

1.	Discuss why managers in the hospitality and tourism industries need to appreciate cultural differences in communication.

2.	Identify the key skills of an effective communicator and suggest how a manager in the hospitality or tourism industries can improve their listening skills.

3.	Discuss the extent to which good communication skills make a good manager.

Practical exercises:

1.	Assess your personal barriers to an accepting attitude when you listen to others (C: 4 p 99).

2.	Evaluate how supportive your body messages are when you listen to others (C: 4 p 104)

3.	Evaluate how supportive your voice messages are when you listen to others (C: 4 p 107).

4.	Compare and contrast the communication skills of two colleagues and identify areas for improvement.

5
RESPONDING

INTRODUCTION

In the previous chapter the importance of listening to others was emphasized. For people working in the hospitality and tourism industries good interpersonal skills are essential and as well as listening carefully to customers and colleagues it is important that they respond positively to requests, comments and advice.

Responding to others positively is a result of rewarding listening. An important aspect of effective communication is confirming to the transmitter that the message has been understood. Difficulties occur sometimes when, due to emotional barriers, an individual is unable to hear what is being said and as a result feels alienated. Controlling inner feelings requires a degree of self-discipline but allows the individual to respond to others effectively. The purpose of this chapter is to review the steps which can be taken by individuals to ensure they respond to others as effectively as possible.

In this chapter:
- Reflective responding (C: 5 pp 112-115)
- Rephrasing (C: 5 pp 115-117; D: 5 p 74)
- Reflecting feelings (C: 5 pp 118-119)
- Identifying feelings, words and phrases (C: 5 pp 119-120)
- Understanding voice and body messages (C: 5 pp 120-122)
- Reflecting feelings from messages (C: 5 pp 122-124)
- Underlying reasons (C: 5 pp 124-125)
- Techniques for reflective responding (C: 5 pp 125-130)
- Confrontation (B: 6 p 122; C: 5 pp 133-134)
- Confrontation methods (B: 6 p 122; C: 5 pp 134-136)

REVIEW

Reflective responding (C: 5 pp 112-115)
When an individual responds to another with understanding they are in fact mirroring their verbal, voice and body messages and identifying the central meaning of the messages. An example of reflective responding is a follows:
Receptionist: 'I have been working in this hotel for three years now and I want to develop my experience and gain promotion.'

Personnel manager: 'You are determined to be a front office manager and are not going to stay in the same job when you no longer feel it challenges you.'

A good reflective response consists of three stages. Firstly a statement is made and this is followed by the reflective response and then a second statement is made. Ideally the second statement should be a continuation of the train of thought embedded in the first comment.

Reflective responding is not an easy skill for everyone to learn and it is not always appropriate but there are situations when the process should be followed and these include:

- *Demonstrating understanding.* It may be necessary to check that a set of instructions have been understood. For example a tour guide taking a group of students on a visit to Windsor will need to check that the group has understood the programme for the day.
- *Helping others to make decisions.* This may occur when a hotel manager is considering the allocation of budgets to different departments.
- *Clarifying another's position.* Where a disagreement arises it is important to establish what the other person thinks and feels about the situation. For example an airline steward dealing with a complaint from a passenger about the quality of a meal.
- *Helping others to express their thoughts and feelings.* A member of staff who is upset because they have not passed a training course may need assistance to identify how they feel as a result of their disappointment.
- *Trying to manage personal problems.* Individuals will often be experiencing personal problems which affect their working lives. It may therefore be necessary to help people to manage these problems.

It should be noted that there will also be occasions when reflective responding is not appropriate. For example when praise is expressed it would lead to embarrassment if a reflective response was used. Other times when reflective responding should be used carefully are when:

- An individual talks too much and the communication needs to become two-way;
- It is important that an individual's internal viewpoint is shared;
- Another's recommendations may be damaging.

Rephrasing (C: 5 pp 115-117; D: 5 p 74)
Good listening involves checking the understanding of the message and the accuracy of the interpretation.

Repeating exactly what the other person has just said is a rather mechanical process and can be frustrating for the speaker. In order to provide an effective reflective response it is necessary to re-word or paraphrase the statement using similar language. In following this procedure it is possible for the receiver to reflect the feelings that have been transmitted and to negotiate over the interpretation of the contents and feelings.

Re-wording can sometimes improve the original statement by making it easier to understand. Speakers often show their appreciation of this technique by making comments such as 'That's exactly the point'. At all stages of the process it is important that voice and body messages are also accurately reflected. The following are examples of how comments may be rephrased: 'I appreciate the help you have given me' could be reworded as a reflective response to become: 'You are grateful for my assistance'. In a similar way the phrase: 'I find it difficult to show positive feelings' could be re-worded as: 'You have trouble expressing affection'.

Reflecting feelings (C: 5 pp 118-119)
Understanding others is achieved, in part, by identifying their feelings and this involves flowing with the emotions expressed by another individual and communicating this back to them. Reflecting feelings encompasses both receiver and sender skills. The following are examples of receiver skills:
• Understanding another's face and body messages;
• Sensing the hidden meaning of another's messages;
• Understanding voice messages.

Sender skills include:
• Re-wording feelings appropriately using expressive language;
• Checking the accuracy of understanding;
• Responding in a manner which relates to another's feelings, words and phrases.

One of the dangers of too much reflective responding is that people may feel sorry for themselves. It is, therefore, important to carefully assess when and when not to reflect feelings. One way to overcome this problem is to add a question such as: 'what could you do to improve your situation?'

Identifying feelings, words and phrases
(C: 5 pp 119-120)
Sometimes the words which people use do not necessarily truly reflect their voice and body messages. For example, a manager hearing she is being transferred by her company to a hotel in another part of the country may say she is pleased

but her voice may sound upset and her face look disappointed. Some words and phrases express feelings more than others. The words in italics in the following examples could be described as 'feelings words': 'I find being without a job *depressing*. I am young and *want to get ahead*. Right now my prospects *look bleak*'. '*Who does he think* he is telling me what to do? If I *didn't need the job* I would tell him to *get lost*.'

Understanding voice and body messages
(C: 5 pp 120-122)
As a listener the individual needs to receive information in a way that shows emotional responsiveness to speakers. This means mirroring voice and body messages - varying voice inflections and facial expressions. It is possible to look sad but at the same time show warmth and sympathy in the voice. Reflective feelings should be accurate in two ways. Firstly feelings must be correctly identified and secondly the level of the intensity of the feelings needs to be correctly expressed. Another factor which should be considered is the extent to which the speaker is prepared to recognise their feelings. For example as a listener an employee may infer that a front office manager is autocratic. The manager may not be able to cope with such a view as it interferes with their self-image of being a democratic leader. It is, therefore, a question of judgement how much feelings are reflected. Children express their emotions openly whereas adults are more careful about when and how they show their emotions. The messages delivered by adults are usually encoded and need to be decoded.

Reflecting feelings from messages
(C: 5 pp 122-124)
Some people communicate their feelings clearly with supporting verbal, voice and body messages. Other individuals have difficulty in expressing their feelings. For example the style of communication adopted may interfere with the effectiveness of what is being said. This situation could arise if less intensity of feeling is communicated than is actually felt. There are a range of factors which can affect the transmission of clear feelings messages which depend on the:
• Situation;
• Person to whom the communication is being directed;
• Gender of the individual;
• Cultural influences;
• Attention of the listener and
• Mood of the sender.

Ideally an individual should try and decode the total message and then develop an emotionally expressive reflective response that demonstrates the theme of

the sender's feelings. Technically it is better to reflect feelings at the beginning of the response.
The following is an example:

Caroline has just lost an important conference booking. Caroline's verbal message is: 'I have just made a major error and as a result the conference booking for three hundred people has gone to our number one competitor. I am so annoyed with myself'. Caroline's voice message: quiet voice, emphasis on 'so annoyed', voice lowers and trails away for 'with myself', sighs. Caroline's body message: down at mouth, pale, tearful, slouched posture, moves slowly. Possible reflection of feeling: 'You are very upset with yourself'.

The reflection of feeling is said a little tentatively to ascertain whether Caroline considers it accurate. The reflection of feeling should be conveyed in a kind voice and body messages should demonstrate interest and attention.

Where there is an element of doubt about the interpretation of the speaker's feelings the response should be more tentative e.g. 'I think you are feeling disappointed with the bar sales for this month - am I right?'

Underlying reasons (C: 5 pp 124-125)
Reflective responding focusing on feelings and causes can help an individual to move forward and develop action. For example, if a manager says he/she is worried about an appraisal interview because the person feels that his/her future with the company depends on it, a reflective response would consider all that has been said including the concerns about the future. By discussing the concerns it should be possible to develop recommendations.

Techniques for reflective responding
(C:5 pp 125-130)
Listening to others is not always possible but in general the process helps others to open up and blossom. Often individuals involved in everyday conversation are not particularly helpful in encouraging others to share their internal viewpoint. An exception is the role of the counsellor where the client is listened to very carefully.

Counsellors are trained to help people to feel safe and secure. Before individuals can reveal their inner thoughts and feelings they require psychological safety and space. If an individual is not accessible or they dominate the conversation or keep interrupting, they are not giving another the quantity of safety and space they need. Further, the quality of safety and space can be affected by showing lack of respect for the importance of their internal viewpoint.

This makes it difficult for people to talk for fear of being 'put down'. The following approaches should be avoided if an individual wants to be a rewarding listener, although there will be occasions when they are necessary:

- *Directing and leading.* Taking control of what another individual can talk about.
- *Judging and evaluating.* Making statements which imply the actions of the other person are being judged.
- *Blaming.* Accusing others of being responsible for a particular problem or difficult situation.
- *Becoming aggressive.* Making comments which attempt to upset another individual.
- *Moralizing.* Telling others how they should lead their lives in a patronizing way.
- *Advising.* Implying that others should do as they are told and not giving them time to make their own decisions.
- *Ignoring another's feelings.* Not appreciating that others have different feelings.
- *Talking about self.* Dominating the conversation by discussing your own feelings.
- *Interrogating.* Questioning others in a way that can be interpreted as threatening.
- *Reassuring.* Ignoring the real feelings of others and trying to make them feel better for your own sake more than theirs.
- *Labelling.* Attempting to diagnose feelings when not qualified to do so.
- *Over-interpreting.* Analyzing another individual and their feelings from an external viewpoint.
- *Distracting.* Confusing the issue by creating a smokescreen.
- *Faking interest.* Pretending to be more interested in what is being said than is really the situation.
- *Time pressures.* Indicating to the speaker that there is not much time available for listening to them.
- *Breaking confidences.* It is important to avoid passing on information which has been given in confidence.

Confrontation (B:6 p 122; C: 5 pp 133-134)
Each person has their own perceptions. Sometimes a challenge or confrontation from outside invites them to review an aspect of their functioning, and as a result broaden and deepen their horizons. Egan (1) views confrontation as an invitation to another to examine his or her style of relating and its consequences for self and others.

There are two different types of confrontation. The first concerns inconsistencies either between what people say and how they say it or what they say and what they do. The second form of confrontation concerns distortions of reality.

In such situations an individual may make comments like: 'They are all out to get me' or 'I'm no good at anything'. An element of judgement is required when dealing with distortions of reality. For example should the listener continue or confront the distortions of reality?

Confrontation methods

(B: 6 p 122; C: 5 pp 134-136)
The approach taken when confronting others is an important consideration. Ideally the confrontation should begin with a reflective response to engage the attention of the other individual and keep them listening. The confrontation should not be any stronger than is necessary to achieve the goal. Heavy and insensitive confrontations can create resistance and upset the individual concerned. Where confrontation is used skilfully the outcome can be very positive with the individual developing and moving forwards. When confronting inconsistencies one approach is to say: 'On the one hand you say... but on the other hand ...' This helps to focus on the differences and develop a solution. When confronting possible distortions of reality the type of statement made, for example, could be: 'You say .. but where is the evidence?' Here the intention is to assist the speaker in producing their own evidence to support their version of reality (2). Wherever possible speakers should be encouraged to confront themselves as this usually leads to less resistance. The style of the confrontation should be democratic so as to avoid any feeling of being put down from developing. Likewise threatening voice and body messages should be persistently challenged as this can harm the relationship.

CONCLUSION

Reflective listening is based on mirroring the essence of the speaker's verbal, voice and body messages so that they feel accurately understood. Reflective responding is achieved by re-wording, decoding and reflecting back feelings and reflecting back the speaker's reasons for their feelings. Confrontation can take two forms: inconsistencies and distortions of reality and both should be managed carefully.

References:

1.   G.Egan. *You and Me: The Skills of Communicating and Relating to Others.* Monterey, CA: Brooks/Cole, 1977.
2.   A.T. Beck & G. Emery. *Anxiety Disorders and Phobias: A Cognitive Perspective.* New York: Basic Books, 1985.

Review questions:

1.   To what extent do you consider managers in the hospitality and tourism industries need good reflective response skills?

2.   Identify three occasions when a hospitality or tourism manager may find themselves in confrontation with others. Suggest how the manager should deal with these three situations to overcome the difficulties.

2.   Explain why an individual may interrogate others or ignore their feelings.

EXTENSION

Read: Chapter 6 of *People and the Hotel and Catering Industry* (D: 6 pp 82-101)

This chapter outlines the factors which affect interpersonal relationships and describes the roles which people adopt. The chapter also discusses the different approaches to social skills training and concludes with an example of customer relations training in a hotel company.

Extension questions:

1.   Discuss why hospitality and tourism managers need to understand the complexity of interpersonal behaviour.

2.   Select three problems which can arise with adopted roles and provide three examples from the hospitality or tourism industries for each problem. Suggest ways in which these difficulties could be overcome.

3.   Discuss the extent to which social skills can be taught.

Practical exercises:

1.   Indicate what voice and body messages might serve as cues for a range of feelings (C: 5 p 122)

2.   Assess the extent to which you consider yourself 'safe' to talk to (C: 5 p 129)

3.   Record what happens when you use confronting skills (C: 5 p 136)

4.   Compare and contrast the response skills of two colleagues and identify areas for improvement.

6
PRESENTING

INTRODUCTION

"Speaking well is thinking clearly. Speaking exceptionally well is thinking exceptionally clearly."
J. Valenti, *Speak up with Confidence: How to Prepare, Learn, and Deliver Effective Speeches*, William Morrow, New York, 1982.

Most people are nervous about giving a presentation to a group whether they be colleagues, customers or members of the public. Becoming a good speaker can only be achieved with practise and hard work. The purpose of this chapter is to identify the stages that should be followed in preparing and delivering a presentation and to help individuals overcome any difficulties they may experience during this process.

In this chapter:
- The purpose of a presentation (E: 36 p 619)
- Understanding the audience (E: 36 pp 619-620)
- Collecting information (E: 36 pp 620-621)
- Preparing the material for delivery (B:7 pp 158-163; E: 36 pp 620-622; F: 3 pp 50-51)
- Speech anxiety (B: 7 pp 141-158)
- Use of audio-visual aids (B: 7 163-167; E: 36 pp 622- 626)
- Delivering the presentation (B: 7 pp 167-176; E: 36 pp 622-629 F: 3 pp 52-53)

REVIEW

The purpose of a presentation (E: 36 p 619)
In essence a presentation is given either to provide the audience with information or to motivate them to take some form of action or both. For example a contract caterer may be providing a group of prospective clients with information about the type of service his company could provide. A food and beverage manager in a hotel may have to give his/her staff information about the requirements of new hygiene legislation. In another situation the head housekeeper of a country house hotel may give a presentation to staff with the aim of improving standards of cleanliness.

Understanding the audience (E: 36 pp 619-620)
The audience may consist of individuals known to the speaker. For example a food and beverage manager in a hotel addressing staff about the introduction of a new menu, or a health and safety officer in a leisure centre informing staff about new accident procedures. Alternatively there may be occasions when an individual is required to give a presentation to people they have never met before. Whether or not the speaker knows the audience does not affect the general principles of delivering a successful presentation but there will be some small differences in approach. For example a representative from the English Tourist Board speaking at a conference in Paris will want to present a positive image of England as a tourist destination. In another situation a training officer running an induction programme for new staff will need to ensure that the trainees are not overloaded with information and that key points are emphasized.

It is important to appreciate that any audience is a collection of individuals with different sets of experience and knowledge. It is therefore advisable to gather as much information about the audience as possible before planning the content of the presentation. A decision then needs to be taken regarding where to pitch the presentation. As a general rule it is wise to aim the talk at those with the least knowledge of the topic being discussed. To meet the needs of those with more knowledge and expertise of the subject, questions can be invited at the end of the presentation.

Collecting information (E: 36 pp 620-621)
Initially the aim should be to collect as much information as possible about the subject of the presentation. The information may be gathered from inside the organization e.g. the marketing manager of a holiday park reviewing sales histories for a talk she is preparing on improving chalet bookings. Sometimes information will be acquired from external sources e.g. the personnel manager of a fast food chain may require information on new employment legislation and will contact a professional body for help. On other occasions it may be necessary to gather information from customers or competitors by undertaking a market research survey. Having gathered sufficient data on which to base the presentation the next step involves sorting and analyzing the material. It may be necessary to convert data into visual information such as tables, graphs or charts.

Preparing the material for delivery
(B: 7 pp 158-163; E: 36 pp 620-622; F: 3 pp 50-51)
Good preparation helps an individual to speak with confidence. The first step involves establishing clear goals concerning the material to be delivered. Ideally a presentation will last approximately twenty minutes - this is the maximum time for which people can usually concentrate.

During the twenty minute period three or five points should be focused on - any more than this and the audience would not remember the key messages of the presentation. Sometimes the objectives are too ambitious and as a result the speaker tries to cover too much material, so when preparing a talk it is helpful to try to think like the listeners (1).

When preparing the presentation, attention should be given to the structure and in particular the introduction and conclusion. The introduction should have three objectives: (a) to create a relationship with the audience or develop it; (b) stimulate the interest and attention of the audience and (c) communicate the aims of the presentation.

The introduction should put the presentation into context and explain, in outline, the material to be covered. In addition the audience should be informed why the presentation is important. Wherever possible the speaker should give examples and introduce some humour into the session.

The language used should take into account the background and knowledge of the audience. For example, the financial manager of a restaurant chain, giving a presentation to unit managers on budgetary control, should avoid using jargon which they may not understand. Likewise the presenter should avoid using too many words as this can block the communication process.

A successful presentation leaves individuals feeling they have gained something from the session. For example a practical presentation concentrating on the preparation of cocktails should aim to present the skills required so that individuals feel confident to undertake the task themselves. In presenting the skills it is necessary to:

- Break the task down;
- Relate the session to the experiences of the audience;
- Give a clear demonstration;
- Ask questions.

It is important to complete the presentation with a good conclusion which summarizes the main points and allows time for questions and, where appropriate, discussion.

The use of notes during the presentation should be considered carefully. Experienced speakers may not need notes to aid their memory because they are very familiar with the content of their presentation. Experienced speakers are also less likely to suffer from anxiety and therefore, loss of concentration.

At the other extreme some individuals prefer to read from a script. Whilst this means the speaker is well prepared, it also leads to a rather wooden presentation which prevents the speaker from having contact with the audience. The approach most speakers adopt is to use notes as memory joggers - this provides back-up but allows the speaker to relate to the audience.

Speech anxiety (B: 7 pp 141-158)
Some people become nervous prior to giving a presentation and as a result suffer speech anxiety. For some, this may be a problem which affects them in a range of interpersonal situations, whereas for others it will be a problem which only occurs when they have to speak in public (2).

When a person suffers speech anxiety they experience a range of feelings, thoughts and reactions. For example a hotel manager giving a presentation to a group of eighty travel agents may feel tense and shaky. It is likely that he will be thinking he is not a good speaker and yet at the same time he will be keen to make the perfect speech.

There are a number of verbal, voice and body action messages which indicate speech anxiety. These messages include not stating own opinions, speaking very quietly and poor eye contact. Sometimes individuals take defensive roles and behave aggressively or act the clown. It should also be noted that some people may cause speech anxiety in others, notably strangers, older people or figures of authority. In a similar way situations are sometimes anxiety-evoking e.g. participating in a discussion group.

The challenge for an individual who suffers speech anxiety is learning how to overcome the problem. There are a number of steps which can be taken to improve the situation (3). The first step involves the underlying feelings of insecurity which lead to the speech anxiety. The individual also needs to use self-talk constructively. This includes keeping calm and breaking tasks down - in essence being in control of the situation. Such a process requires a good deal of effort and practice.

Everyone has a set of inner rules which shape the direction of their lives. These rules can be either self-supporting or self-oppressing. In some cases an individual may oppress themself through inappropriate personal rules. For example the person who feels they must give a perfect presentation should try and overcome these feelings by asking 'what is the worst thing that might happen if I give a less than perfect talk'?

It is important that individuals perceive themselves accurately and engage in 'positive asset search' to identify their strengths (4). In the same way it is important to perceive others accurately. People frequently have automatic thoughts and perceptions that influence their emotions (5).

In an attempt to explain their speech anxiety individuals sometimes try to attribute the problem to a range of causes. These include unfortunate experiences in their past, blaming the audience and feeling it is all their fault. These explanations are often part of the problem and it is important that individuals do not view these as insurmountable.

Use of audio-visual aids
(B: 7 pp 163-167; E: 36 pp 622-626)
Visual aids help to increase audience attention and emphasize the key points of the presentation. It should be noted, however, that visual aids are supplementary and not a replacement for the talk. There are a wide range of visual aids in use today. These include slides, overhead transparencies, flip charts, videos, photographs and samples e.g. new products. There are disadvantages and advantages for using each visual aid. For example using an overhead projector enables the speaker to prepare transparencies in advance. The transparencies should not be overloaded with information and if possible should be typed to give a professional image. When using an overhead it is important to check the controls and the positioning of the projector and screen before using it. Flip charts are a useful aid as sheets can be prepared in advance and can be retained as a record after the session. Flip charts are particularly useful when running a brainstorming session for example. Visual aids such as cartoons can be used to introduce some humour into the presentation and emphasize key messages.

Delivering the presentation
(B: 7 167-176; E: 36 pp 626-629; F: 3 pp 52-53)
The delivery of a good presentation demands particular skills. Time and energy needs to be invested in the preparation of the delivery. The skills are based on four 'Ps': preparing, practising, polishing and persuading. Preparation involves checking on timing and polishing involves the fine tuning of the content. Persuading is one of the aims of the presentation - to convince the audience to take some form of action.

Developing voice awareness requires breaking down the voice communication into its principal component skills. The acronym VAPER represents these skills:

- *Volume.* This should not be too loud or too quiet as either will cause difficulties for the audience.

- *Articulation.* Words should be enunciated clearly and mumbling should be avoided.

- *Pitch.* Anxiety usually leads to a higher pitch of voice.

- *Emphasis.* The speaker needs to convey interest and commitment to the audience. It is important to avoid being a monotonous speaker.

- *Rate.* Nervous speakers tend to talk too quickly. A slower speech rate helps individuals to control their nerves and gives them time to think. Pauses act as a form of punctuation and they can be used to give the audience time to think about what is being said and to record notes.

When addressing an audience it is also important to convey effective body messages. The acronym GAME represents the key body message components:

- *Gesture and facial expression.* There are three main types of gesture which can aid the expression of ideas and feelings (6). These are emphatic, descriptive and symbolic gestures. An example of an emphatic gesture is pointing the finger to indicate importance. Descriptive gestures include using the arms to illustrate two opposing points of view. A symbolic gesture would be shaking the head to show disagreement with a view. It should be noted that gestures should be sensitive to cultural differences. This is very important for those working in the hospitality and tourism industries where both staff and customers are often international. Facial expressions can help to illustrate ideas and feelings. A nervous speaker may look strained whilst a relaxed presenter will be smiling.

- *Appearance.* Both dress and hairstyle can help to give a positive image to the speaker and create an air of authority where necessary.

- *Movement and posture.* Bad speakers tend to have distracting movements e.g. pacing up and down whereas good speakers stand relaxed and comfortable.

- *Eye contact.* Good eye contact draws the audience into the presentation and enables the speaker to assess reactions.

Once the presentation has been delivered the speaker may be required to deal with questions from the audience. In order to manage this part of the session effectively the speaker should prepare answers to the obvious questions in advance and reply to the whole group. The speaker should never be tempted to make up an answer if it is based on guess work.

CONCLUSION

Hospitality and tourism managers frequently find themselves in a position where they are required to give a presentation to a small group or a large audience. It is therefore essential that they are confident in public speaking. This chapter has highlighted the need for thorough preparation and effective delivery skills if a presentation is to be successful. It is important that goals are set and that clear language is used. The talk should also be supported by positive body messages. Where appropriate audio visual aids may be included in the presentation to emphasize key points and introduce variety into the delivery.

References:

1. D. Bernstein, *Put It Together, Put It Across: The Craft of Business Presentations.* Cassell, London 1988.
2. D.H. Meichenbaum, J.B. Gilmore & A. Fedoravicius, 'Group Insight Versus Group Desensitization in Treating Speech Anxiety', *Journal of Consulting and Clinical Psychology,* 36, 410-21, 1971.
3. R. Nelson-Jones, *Effective Thinking Skills: Preventing and Managing Personal Problems.* Cassell, London, 1989.
4. A.E. Ivey, M.B. Ivey & L. Simek-Downing. *Counselling and Psychotherapy: Integrating skills, Theory and Practice* (2nd edition), Prentice-Hall, Engelwood Cliffs, NJ, 1987.
5. A.T. Beck & M.E. Weishaar, *Cognitive Therapy* in R. Corsinsi & D. Wedding (eds), *Current Psychotherapies* (4th edition), pp 285-320, Peacock, Itasca, IL, 1989.
6. R.L. Fischer, *Speak to Communicate: An Introduction to Speech.* Dickenson Publishing Company, Encino, C.A, 1972.

Review questions:

1. From your own experience describe a poor presentation. What were the underlying reasons for this?

2. Identify your own strengths and weaknesses when giving a presentation.

3. To what extent do you think new technology will remove the need for personal presentations in the future?

EXTENSION

Read: Chapter 9 of *Personal Effectiveness* (F: 9 pp 198-222)

This chapter explores the wider meaning of communication when it is applied to organizations which aim to transmit messages to potential or actual customers. The discussion includes a review of market research techniques, the delivery of sales presentations, the role of advertising and public relations and other marketing communications.

Extension questions:

1. Discuss the occasions when a hospitality or tourism manager may be required to give a sales presentation. Identify the key components of such a presentation.

2. Explore the differences between giving a presentation to a group of potential customers and a staff meeting to outline changes in the organization structure.

3. Discuss the value of advertising and public relations for the hospitality and tourism industries.

Practical exercises:

1. Assess your own level of speech anxiety (B: 7 p 144)

2. Develop your voice skills (B: 7 pp 169-170)

3. Prepare a ten minute presentation on a topic of your choice related to hospitality or tourism management. Deliver the presentation and request constructive feedback from your audience. What did you learn from this exercise?

4. Undertake a survey of your group to determine the ingredients of a successful presentation. Prepare a report on your findings.

7
TEAMS AND GROUPS

INTRODUCTION

"Management is no longer about running an assembly line of sequential processes, but about giving assignments to groups of people committed to bringing them to a successful conclusion within a specific time. It's like winning a game."
Paul Thorne, industrial psychologist, cited in (1).

A key criterion for the selection of managers in hospitality and tourism organizations is the ability to organize, motivate and relate to teams or groups of individuals. Managers in turn, aim to recruit staff who can contribute to the particular blend of personalities, talents and experiences, needed to maximize team effectiveness. This chapter seeks to explore these issues.

The hospitality and tourism industries face rapidly changing economic, social, political and technological conditions. In these circumstances, change and innovation needs to be more continuous than it has been in the past and these processes depend heavily on team and group members solving problems both invididually and collectively.

In this chapter:
*   What is a team or group?
    (D: 7 pp 102-104; E: 33 pp 594-595)
*   The structure of teams and groups
    (D: 7 pp 104-106; E: 33 pp 599-601) (2)
*   Team-building: The development of teams and groups (D: 7 pp 106-117; E: 33 pp 595-602)

REVIEW

What is a team or group?
(D: 7 pp 102-104; E: 33 pp 594-595)
A group is a combination of two or more people aiming to achieve common objectives. The term 'group' can embrace the activities of many organizational stakeholders such as: (a) consumers; (b) employees; (c) managers; (d) shareholders; (e) suppliers; (f) proprietors; (g) companies and (h) government officials.

Groups are either *formal* (structures and behaviours bound by specific rules and predetermined agendas) or *informal* (spontaneous, ad hoc, self-determined).

They may or may not involve superior-subordinate relationships. There are three basic types of groups: (a) task or project; (b) functional and (c) friendship or interest groups.

(a) Task or project group. This is established for a specific period of time to accomplish stated objectives. It is normally formal in nature with a superior-subordinate structure relating to the nature of the work to be completed. For example, a squad of football players who are chosen to represent their country in the world cup.

(b) Functional group. This is a formal group whose composition, objectives and activities are determined by superiors within the organization. For example, a team of assistants in a fast food outlet perform tasks as instructed by their supervisor or unit manager, who in turn receives orders from her regional manager, ultimately is responsible to head office.

(c) Friendship or *interest groups.* These groupings which are based on shared interests, values or beliefs may be formal or informal and can exist within or externally to an organizational structure. For example, a catering society set up by students to promote social and cultural activities amongst its members might function autonomously or as part of a college's alumni network.

While 'group' embraces all three of the preceding categories, the concept of a 'team' applies more to the first category of task or project. Hence, a squad of footballers constitute a group as they prepare, but it is a 'team' of players that seeks to achieve the objective of winning the football match.

The structure of teams and groups
(D: 7 pp 104-106; E: 33 pp 599-601) (2)
Team and group structures can be described in terms of six components: (i) group composition; (ii) norms; (iii) roles; (iv) status; (v) cohesiveness and (vi) leadership.

(i) Group composition.
Groups are either *homogeneous* (people of similar personality, attitude, and motivation) or *heterogeneous* (people of mixed characteristics). Both have their uses, for example a travel service firm sends a team of people on a public relations tour of large organizations to gain new business. A united, positive and confident approach is called for and so a homogeneous team is required. The same firm is seeking to establish branches for its operations in South East Asia and an imaginative strategy is required, given the different and less familiar political and economic environment.

A heterogeneous group is formed to stimulate ideas and promote a rich discussion of alternatives.

How should applicants or nominees be screened and selected for a specific team? One approach which is currently in vogue is to send employees on an outward bound course. There is some evidence to suggest that under testing conditions, people revert to their true personality type and natural leaders emerge, though they are not necessarily the same people that hold managerial or supervisory positions in the work environment.

(ii) Norms.

Norms are rules that define the form of behaviour permitted in a group. They are determined by the members of the group or by the organization or institution that controls the group. Norms provide a code of conduct by which each individual can gauge and relate to the behaviour of other members and may be implied or explicitly stated. For example, it is a norm when providing silver service in a restaurant for male staff to wear dark suits, black shoes, white shirts and a tie or bow tie.

(iii) Roles.

Roles are established sets of actions and behaviours and individuals within a group are expected to behave in accordance with the role that has been specified by his/her manager or supervisor. There are three types of role:

- *Expected* - defined as the actions, behaviours and activities that are required by a particular job or task as prescribed by a job description;

- *Perceived* - defined by what the person doing the job or task believes is required and/or important;

- *Enacted* - defined by the way in which the person doing the job or task actually behaves while undertaking the work.

An individual may experience *role ambiguity* (uncertainty about his or her authority, responsibility, job duties) or *role conflict* (being asked to perform two or more roles at the same time). For example, a part-time waiter who is also a single father, finds himself experiencing role conflict when he is required to pick his child up from nursery school at the same time as he is required at work to lay tables. At work, he then experiences role ambiguity when he finds that as well as serving food, he is also expected to wash dishes and on occasions be the cashier.

(iv) Status.

Status refers to how the individual is regarded or rated compared to others in the group. Status may, for instance be conferred on the holder of a particular post, be based on educational qualifications or reflect the particular skills required in the job. It may also reflect personality or background. Problems occur when there is disagreement about an individual's status, or when people behave, or carry out tasks, that are inconsistent with their status. For example, a management graduate is about to commence employment with a large hotel. There is disagreement among senior management. Some prefer the graduate to learn the hard way by spending time doing every job in the hotel; others see this as a waste of talent and want the person to be deployed in a management capacity from the outset.

(v) Cohesiveness.

Cohesiveness is a measure of the interpersonal relationships between members. Cohesion implies effective communication, co-operation and joint effort towards achieving group goals.

(vi) Leadership.

Leadership may be *formal* or *informal*. A formal leader is given authority and power from management to control a group. An informal leader is given authority by the members themselves. The current vogue is for *self-directed teams* based on the idea that leadership rotates naturally to the person best qualified to run specific parts of the task.

Team-building: The development of teams and groups (D: 7 pp 106-117; E: 33 pp 594-602)
Team-building is concerned with the process of removing obstacles that may prevent the team functioning effectively and with finding ways of improving the team's overall performance. Tackman (3) suggests that groups tend to go through four distinctive stages:

- *Stage 1 - forming* (mutual acceptance) when members meet for the first time and establish communication patterns. Goals and expectations are discussed. Interdependence develops as members begin to accept one another.
- *Stage 2 - storming* (communication and decision-making) when goals and ground rules are determined and patterns of interpersonal relationships develop.
- *Stage 3 - norming* (growth and productivity) when an effective communication network between group members is established. This facilitates cohesion and good interpersonal relations as members work constructively towards the attainment of group goals.

- *Stage 4 - performing* (control and organization) when appraisal and evaluation helps to facilitate tasks. The group revises and renews its interdependence and remains well motivated towards goal attainment.

According to Jacobs and Everett (4) most management teams tend to operate in both a co-operative and a political way. Further, they are successful at solving puzzles where solutions already exist and need to be found, but less successful at solving problems where nobody knows what the answer is. If problem-solving is to be effective, genuine team behaviour is essential and this requires: (a) openness with each other; (b) a willingness to express feelings; (c) trust; (d) an ability to formulate shared objectives; (e) a readiness to work through conflict situations that may arise; (f) commitment; (g) a willingness to develop and use appropriate interpersonal skills and (h) a consensus style of decision-making.

Managers can learn valuable lessons from the playing field, for instance, that purchasing talent does not guarantee success. On the sports field, players are asssigned positions but their tasks are defined by their role in the game plan, not by their position. Belbin noticed the same thing was true of the business teams that were most successful in producing solutions to case studies. Members of a team seek out certain roles and they perform most effectively in the ones that are natural to them. (5) Belbin created nine categories of roles, 'nine' also being the number he regarded as the optimum for a project team. It is headed by a co-ordinator whose role corresponds to that of a company chairperson and by the task leader who acts out the role of chief executive by shaping and driving the team. Other roles include the ideas person, the doer, the organizer, the critic and the specialist who has subject expertise. The value of Belbin's analysis is that it helps to isolate the weaknesses as well as the strengths of each member of the team. A barrier to successful team-building is 'over-conformity' which leads to what has been labelled as *groupthink*. This involves:

- Shared stereotypes about people or groups outside;
- Protecting the leader against information that conflicts with the group's aims or values;
- An illusion of invulnerability;
- Self-censorship - members hold back from saying things that might conflict with commonly held views;
- An illusion of unanimity - a belief that everyone is in agreement.

This type of conformity is more likely to be found in longstanding, highly cohesive groups. Groupthink leads to the more creative people being seen as 'non-conformist minorities', their creativity, innovation and originality being ignored because they do not conform sufficiently to group values and norms. One strategy that has proved helpful in easing conformity is based on the theory of *career anchors*. An anchor is a set of key work and career preferences that people hang on to because they provide continuity and stability when taking critical decisions. For example, people anchored by the desire for 'autonomy' are more likely to perform at their best in small autonomous operations, such as consultancies. A team's identity and the underlying values that help create it are critical to the way a team defines and judges effective performance. Generally, managers who develop the same anchor or identity as the team are seen by the team as more effective than those with a different anchor.

A key issue for executive team development is how to overcome the barriers created by the inherent conservatism of teams. The answer lies in raising awareness of performance issues and establishing a way for team members to talk openly. The steps involved are:

- Identify individual anchors and construct a team identity map (identify any dominant coalitions of the same or similar anchors).
- Construct a team assessment questionnaire by identifying the most important performance indicators for the team. The items are then included in a questionnaire to be completed by every member.
- Every member of the team rates the performance of other members of the team, including themselves, against the list of performance statements.
- Analyze the data to see how much shared perception there is about individual performance.
- Provide feedback and counselling for the individual and team.

The aim of the exercise is to stimulate a greater awareness among members of the group about key issues, to identify areas of strength and shortfall in the team as a whole and to begin planning any future action or activities to strengthen individual team performance. These may include: (a) training and development exercises; (b) special projects assigned to sub-groups within the team and (c) developing a commitment to individual counselling either with the consultant or the team leader.

CONCLUSION

Organizations throughout the Western world have been rationalizing and 'down-sizing' their organizational hierarchies. Much of the work of business and industry is now assigned to mobile project management teams, often formed to solve a problem and then disbanded. Accordingly, the manager needs to be flexible and adaptable, creating teams that are most suited to handle whatever problems arise in the ever changing market and technological environment. In turn, teams must be responsive to the needs of the organization and its members. Finally, it is important to note that 'genuine' teams are a prerequisite for productive and innovative organizational activity.

References:

1.   G. Golzen. 'Team Up for Business Success.' *The Sunday Times,* 21 February, 1993, p 42.

2.   R.M. Hodgetts. *Organizational behaviour: Theory and Practice.* Merrill, New York, 1991.

3.   B.W. Tackman. 'Development Sequence in Small Groups.' *Psychological Bulletin,* 1965.

4.   R.C. Jacobs & J.G. Everett, 'The Importance of Team Building in a High Tech Environment.' *Journal of European Industrial Training,* 12 (4) 1988.

5.   M. Belbin. *Management Teams: Why they Succeed or Fail.* Butterworth-Heinemann, London, 1983.

Review questions:

1.   In what circumstances might a person be more likely to conform to the behavioural norms of a work group? If one or more members are reluctant to conform, what can the group leader do in order to create a sense of group identity and unity of purpose?

2.   What forms of role conflict might arise amongst staff in a contract catering unit engaged to provide the catering for the head office of an international bank?

2.   How can '*group think*' lead to decisions being taken which group members don't agree with but are unwilling to voice concern about? How might this situation be resolved?

EXTENSION

Read: Chapter 1 of *Lifeskills: A Handbook.* (B:1 pp 1-23)

This chapter looks at the growth and types of training groups; the skills needed to facilitate such groups; the role of leaders in training groups and it reviews the criticisms made of such groups.

Extension questions:

1.   The manager of a fast food outlet wishes to increase profits and to facilitate this would like to 'get more out of her team'. What particular aspects of group behaviour might she focus on in order to achieve this?

2.   What are the main reasons for the growth of training groups in hospitality and tourism organizations?

3.   Give examples of situations to be found in hospitality and tourism organizations where it it is appropriate to to form a training group. Use B: 1 pp 2-5 as the basis for defining the relationship between the training situation and the type of training group you would recommend.

Practical exercises:

1.   Read B: 1 p. 22. In small groups of two or three, assess your skills as potential training group leaders. First, assess your own skills and potential and then do the same for your colleagues. Compare notes and discuss your observations.

2.   Read E: 33 pp 599-600. Repeat the procedure used in practical exercise 1, this time to assess the team member skills and qualities of your small group.

3.   Next time you attend a meeting, pay close attention to the behaviour of the chairperson. What did he or she do right in running the meeting? What could he or she have done to be more effective? Volunteer to chair a committee at one of the clubs or associations to which you belong. Specifically practice the behaviours you have identified with effectively running a group meeting.

8
MOTIVATION

INTRODUCTION

"All managers have a duty to motivate their teams. Motivated people take more pride in their jobs and work better. But many managers don't know how to motivate their staff". Institute of Management, Management News, No. 64, February 1990, p6.

Understanding what motivates people to work is a difficult task. The role of the manager is to ensure that organizational objectives are achieved by identifying what motivates individual members of staff. Whilst this approach to employee motivation appears relatively simple and straightforward, in reality the process is more complex. This is because all human beings are different and what motivates one does not necessarily motivate another. There are a range of theories which have been developed over time to explain the motivation phenomenon and the purpose of this chapter is to highlight those which are most applicable to the hospitality and tourism industries.

In this chapter:
- Defining motivation (D: 4 p 49; E: 5 p 134; F: 2 p 27; G: 8 pp 197-199)
- Maslow's hierarchy of needs model (D: 4 pp 51-52; E: 3 pp 94-98; F: 2 p 28; G: 8 pp 201-203)
- Herzberg's two-factor theory (D: 4 p 53; E: 5 pp 136-137; G: 8 pp 204-206)
- McGregor's *theory x* and *theory y* (D: 4 pp 52-53; E: 3 pp 98-103; G: 5 pp 116-117)
- Expectancy theories (D: 4 pp 54-55; E: 5 pp 137-139; G: 8 pp 208-212)
- Job design (D:4 pp 57-58; G: 8 pp 215-218)

REVIEW

Defining motivation
(D:4 p 49; E: 5 p 134; F: 2 p 27; G: 8 pp 197-199)
The study of motivation is concerned with the behaviour of individuals and in particular understanding what shapes the direction of their actions. The productivity levels and the quality of work achieved in an organization is determined not only by the competence of the staff but also by the level of motivation. In essence, performance is a function of both ability and the motivation to use ability (1).

One function of management is to encourage staff to realize their full potential by providing them with opportunities to perform well in their work. For example a food and beverage manager could give an experienced waiter the opportunity of training new restaurant staff. This would allow the waiter to develop and grow in his job. It can be said, therefore that motivation arises from the fulfilment of an individual's needs and expectations.

People are motivated in a variety of ways and by various means including money, responsibility and achievement. Social interactions and in particular teamwork are also important for those working in the hospitality and tourism industries. Individuals who are highly motivated demonstrate certain characteristics. These include:

- A committed approach to their work and clear goals;
- An independent outlook and the ability to make their own decisions;
- A desire to be challenged and to achieve high standards.

Understanding what motivates people to work well is a challenge facing all managers. There is no straightforward answer as motivation varies over time and is dependent on individual circumstances. There are, however, a number of theories which managers can use to assist them in creating a motivated team of staff.

Maslow's hierarchy of needs model (D:4 pp 51-52; E: 3 pp 94-98; F: 2 p 28; G: 8 pp 201-203)
Maslow developed the proposition that individuals always want more, and that what they desire depends on what they already have. Malsow suggests that physiological, security/safety, social, ego, and self-realization needs can be arranged in some form of order or hierarchy. Physiological needs are at the lowest level of the hierarchy and include food, water and sleep; self-realization is the highest need and this concerns the development of the individual's personality and the opportunity to maximize abilities and respond to challenges. The basic premise of Maslow's theory is that once a lower-level need has been satisfied it no longer acts as a strong motivator. It should be noted however, that a particular need at one level does not necessarily have to be satisfied fully before the next need develops. As lower-level needs become in the main, satisfied, higher-level needs emerge.

There are some criticisms of Malsow's theory. For example, people cannot always fully satisfy needs and aspirations in their job.

To fully understand what motivates an individual member of staff a manager would need to know about their home and social circumstances as well as their work life. In addition people are not only motivated by their own needs - what other people feel and think affects them. Although the Malsow model is rather simplistic it does provide a helpful background against which to analyze the needs and expectations of people in the work situation.

Herzberg's two-factor theory
(D:4 p 53; E: 5 pp 136-137; G: 8 pp 204-206)
This particular theory links job satisfaction to motivation and puts forward the idea that job satisfaction and job dissatisfaction are dissimilar and reflect different facets of human nature. Factors such as job environment, salary, security, company policy and supervision are categorized as 'hygiene' or 'maintenance' factors by Herzberg. Whilst hygiene factors prevent an individual from being dissatisfied with their job, their presence does not contribute directly to job satisfaction. Using a medical analogy, good hygiene cannot in itself create good health but it can prevent an individual catching a disease. Hygiene factors are particularly relevant to the hospitality and tourism industries where staff who live on the premises and have meals whilst on duty are concerned about their work environment.

In order to increase job satisfaction and therefore motivation, it is necessary to give attention to the 'motivators' or 'growth' factors. These include a sense of achievement, recognition, responsibility, the nature of the job itself, personal growth and advancement. Whilst the motivators do influence the degree of satisfaction experienced by individuals, they do not necessarily contribute to dissatisfaction. In other words, the opposite of dissatisfaction is not necessarily a state of satisfaction but an absence of dissatisfaction.

As with all theories, there are some criticisms. Not all individuals are interested in motivators or growth factors particularly if they are employed on a temporary or casual basis and do not have a high level of commitment towards the organization. Some staff view work as a means to an end and are motivated by money rather than the nature of their job. For others there is no desire for responsibility and they are content to work within a structured work environment.

McGregor's *theory y* and *theory y*
(D: 4 pp 52-53; E: 3 pp 98-103; G: 5 pp 116-117)
McGregor analyzed the behaviour of people at work and developed a set of assumptions which he referred to as theory 'x' and theory 'y'.
Theory x represents the assumptions on which traditional organizations are based, and these are as follows:

- The average person does not like work and will avoid it if he can.
- Most individuals must be coerced, directed and threatened with punishment to make them work towards organization objectives.
- People prefer to be directed and wish to avoid responsibility.
- Individuals generally have little ambition and want security most of all.

In contrast, McGregor developed *theory y* which represents a set of assumptions which are more closely related to the principles of human relations management. They are as follows:

- People enjoy work.
- Individuals will discipline themselves to achieve objectives which they are committed to.
- Commitment to objectives is linked to associated rewards.
- Under appropriate conditions, individuals accept and seek responsibility.
- The capacity for creative problem-solving is widespread amongst members of an organization.
- The abilities of individuals are only partially utilized in organizations.

Theory y depends on the attitude of management towards the creation of opportunities for employee development. This may be achieved by: delegation, participation in decision-making and performance appraisal systems.

Expectancy theories
(D:4 pp 54-55; E: 5 pp 137-139; G: 8 pp 208-212)
The basis of expectancy theories is that individuals are affected by the anticipated results of their actions, including rewards. For example, a leisure centre attendant desires higher status and wants promotion to assistant manager. The desire will only prompt a higher level of performance if the individual feels that there is a strong likelihood that this will lead to promotion - and that promotion will lead to an increase in status.

Vroom's expectancy model is centred on three key variables: (a) valence; (b) instrumentality and (c) expectancy. *Valence* is a measure of the attractiveness or preference to the individual of a particular outcome. *Instrumentality* is concerned with the degree to which performance related outcomes relate to the satisfaction of the need-related outcomes. For some individuals, a higher level of performance may be enough and they may not have further expectations. In the main however, good performance achieves valence as this is central to the satisfaction of second-level outcomes such as promotion. *Expectancy* is the perceived level of probability that the choice of a particular step will actually result in the desired outcome. In essence expectancy is the relationship between a particular course of action and its predicted outcome.

Porter and Lawler put forward a model of motivation which is based on performance as a whole. They maintain that, due to three variables, effort expended does not automatically result in performance improvement:

- *Abilities of the individual.* These include competence, personality and experience.
- *Role perceptions.* The way people view their job and the role they should adopt affects the effort they put in to their work.
- *Intrinsic and extrinsic rewards.* The rewards anticipated have an influence on performance levels.

Porter and Lawler consider that the effort an individual invests in an activity is linked more to motivation than performance and that job satisfaction is a consequence rather than a cause of performance.

Job design (D: 4 pp 57-58; G: 8 pp 215-218)
Herzberg in his theory of motivation illustrates the significance of job design. Through effective job design it is possible to meet an individual's personal and social needs and to maximize the satisfaction that people derive from their work.

There are two facets of job design: content and context. The *content* concerns the tasks that an individual undertakes. For example a room attendant will be responsible for cleaning rooms and making beds. The *context* of the job includes both the physical environment and the social structure in which the job is carried out. For the room attendant this includes the design of the guest rooms, her uniform, her colleagues and the guests she meets.

The basic theory is that if the content and/or context of a job is improved, satisfaction will increase and along with it, the level of productivity. It should be noted however, that the link between improved job content/context is unpredictable. Even so, many organizations choose to redesign jobs either by enlarging or enriching them.

Job enlargement is concerned with increasing the range of tasks that an individual is responsible for. For example, a chef may be given the responsibility for the preparation of a wider range of dishes. In the restaurant, a waiter may be given more tables to serve. Job enlargement is not always popular with staff because it may mean performing a wider range of tasks, but it does facilitate the development of new skills and challenges.

Job enrichment aims to incorporate growth factors such as increased responsibility and opportunities for achievement. Essentially it involves giving individuals greater autonomy and control of their own work in an effort to create a more interesting job. For example, a reservations clerk may be given responsibility for setting booking targets which may provide the added stimulus of an operational goal.

Changing the physical and social environment can affect productivity levels. Past approaches to job redesign have illustrated that technical efficiency, based on the division of labour and task repetition, leads to job dissatisfaction. This dissatisfaction can be overcome by focusing on the social factors inherent in work organizations.

There are other job design techniques which can be employed to improve motivation. These include the creation of autonomous work groups and quality circles. Autonomous work groups are given responsibility for the regulation and organization of their jobs. Goals are established and monitored by the group members. A quality circle is a similar concept, but with an emphasis on problem-solving and continuous quality improvement.

CONCLUSION

The hospitality and tourism industries employ a large number of people and managers should therefore, be aware of what motivates different individuals to perform effectively in their jobs. Given the diversity of the hospitality and tourism industries it is important to focus on the different sub-sectors when developing an approach to staff motivation.

For example in the fast food sector, where the working environment is highly systemized, staff should be trained to undertake a range of tasks so that repetition and routine by job rotation. This also gives added operational flexibility and fosters a sense of teamwork and collective responsibility.

A number of motivation theories have been outlined and reviewed in this chapter, but there are others which help to inform this broad-ranging and important topic, such as the work of Alderfer and McClelland. Alderfer's continuum of needs model reduces Maslow's five levels to three and McClelland's achievement motivation model is based on affiliation , power and achievement.
In attempting to improve employee motivation, organizations tend to focus on job design. This can take the form of enlargement, enrichment, rotation or what is currently referred as employee empowerment.

Finally, the extent to which money is a motivator is considered to be a complex issue. It is generally agreed, however, that individuals are not motivated solely by money e.g. by taking part in voluntary work. In essence, motivating staff can be described as a process of developing a work environment where people willingly put in effort to achieve the aims and objectives of the organization whilst meeting their own needs.

Reference:

1. V.H. Vroom and E.L Deci (eds). *Management and Motivation*. Penguin, 1970.

Review questions:

1. Select three motivation theories and discuss how they could be applied to jobs in a sector of the hospitality or tourism industries.

2. Identify two jobs in the hospitality or tourism industries which you consider to be repetitive and likely to lead to job dissatisfaction. Outline how each job could be re-designed to create an opportunity for improving the motivation levels of staff.

3. Discuss the extent to which money motivates you and your colleagues to work.

EXTENSION

Read: Chapter 4 of *Supervisory Management* (E: 4 pp 112-126)

This chapter concentrates in particular on the role of the supervisor in the organization in terms of defining the work of staff, developing effective working relationships and managing the production of goods and services.

Extension questions:

1. Explore the difficulties that a supervisor may encounter in their role as a 'link person' between the workforce and management.

2. Identify the key skills and knowledge required by a supervisor in a restaurant, travel agency and hotel. To what extent are the skills and knowledge common?

3. In what ways can and should a supervisor motivate his/her staff? What limits or impedes a supervisor's ability to motivate staff?

Practical exercises:

1. Using a tourism or hospitality organization with which you are familiar, interview two members of staff and identify what motivates them to work well. Compare and contrast your findings.

2. Assuming you have been appointed as a head of department in a hospitality or tourism organization and that morale is very low amongst staff. Outline: (a) the steps you would take to overcome the problem and (b) explain how the different motivation theories may influence your actions.

3. Read the 'Burntin Limited' case study (E: 5 p 150, exercise A 5.5) and answer the question.

4. Read the 'Individual Potteries Limited' case study (E: 2 p 111, exercise A 3.2) and answer the questions.

9
LEADING

INTRODUCTION

The concept of leadership has been discussed by management theorists for many years. It has been defined as *"the ability to stimulate people to understand for themselves what they should do and be motivated to do it."* (1) Some of the theories are quite different and others no more than a variation on a theme. The purpose of this chapter is first, to provide an understanding of the leadership role and second, to present the main theories which have been developed over time. The hospitality and tourism industries are people intensive and it is therefore important that managers understand the general principles of effective leadership.

In this chapter:

- Defining leadership (D: 8 pp 120-121; E: 8 p 207; F: 8 p 181; G: 11 p 282)
- The role of the leader (E: 8 pp 208-209; G: 11 pp 287-288)
- Power and influence (F: 8 pp 186-189; G: 11 p 284)
- Characteristics of leaders (E: 8 pp 207-210; F: 8 p 182; G: 11 pp 286-287)
- Action-centred leadership (E: 8 pp 208-209; F: 8 pp 182-183; G: 11 pp 288-290)
- The contingency approach (D: 8 pp 123-124; E: 8 p 210; G: 1 pp 296-299)
- The managerial grid (D: 8 pp 122-123; E: 8 pp 211-213; G: 5 pp 117-119)
- The continuum theory (E: 8 pp 213-214; F: 8 pp 184-185; G:11 pp 294-295)
- Likert (D: 8 pp 124-125; E: 8 p 211; G: 7 pp 185-186)
- Selecting a leadership style (D: 8 pp 125-127; E: 8 pp 214-215; F: 8 p 186; G: 11 pp 302-303)

REVIEW

Defining leadership (D: 8 pp 120-121; E: 8 p 207; F: 8 p 181; G: 11 p 282)
Leadership is a dynamic process whereby an individual is able to influence others to contribute voluntarily to the achievement of group tasks in a given situation. It is a complex activity which is associated with team-building, interpersonal behaviour, communication and motivation. The leader is seen as the focus of the group who enables them to complete a task and to maintain effective work relationships.

The role of the leader
(E: 8 pp 208-209; G: 11 pp 287-288)
The role of the leader varies according to the situation and the nature of the group. In general, however, the leader has a number of functions. For example, he or she plans and establishes goals and objectives for others to achieve. The leader also acts as a controller and mediator dealing with sources of interpersonal conflict among members of the group. In addition, the leader is a source of information and advice and provides a role model of behaviour.

Power and influence (F: 8 pp 186-189; G: 11 p 284)
French and Raven (2) identify five main sources of power on which perceptions of leadership are based:
- *Reward power*. The authority to recommend promotion, pay increases and wider recognition.
- *Coercive power*. The use of sanctions to punish staff who do not comply with directives.
- *Legitimate power*. In this situation the leader's influence is derived from 'position' power and is based on formal authority.
- *Referent power*. Due to respect or charisma, an individual may have influence over others.
- *Expert power*. Specialist, knowledge-based power.

Power relates to the capacity to affect the behaviour of others or the actual ability to undertake and control a given task. It should also be noted that a power equation exists. For example, a manager who decides to punish his staff for not achieving sales targets may find that they decide to work less hard and productivity levels decline further as a result.

Characteristics of leaders
(E: 8 pp 207-210; F: 8 p 182; G: 11 pp 286-287)
A leader may be appointed formally or informally. The formal leader is elected to a particular position by a recognized process. The informal leader emerges from within a group due to their expertise and/or personal qualities.

Early studies of leadership were based on the theory that leaders are born and not made. Attention focused on attempts to identify a set of qualities, attributes or physical characteristics that the 'ideal' leader should possess. These included *physical traits* such as energy and appearance, *personality traits* like adaptability and self-confidence and *social traits* such as interpersonal skills and the ability to work co-operatively with others. Today, it is recognized that good leaders will not necessarily possess all the traits and qualities which were identified as important. Further, there is some evidence that characteristics like dependability and respect for others are behaviours which are more relevant to the role of leader and that these can be learned.

Walker (3) identifies the following qualities as among the most important indicators of an appropriate temperament for leadership:
- Self control
- Consistent values
- Drive
- A consistent level of morale
- Sensitivity
- An ability to support and defend ideas
- Self-awareness

It is difficult to define leadership without identifying the reasons why people are prepared to follow leaders. These include:
- A fear of criticism and/or punishment;
- A desire to obey rules and procedures;
- Respect for a leader's accepted position;
- The earned credibility of the leader.

Current theories favour leadership models which are based on trust and respect. This requires a flexible approach and effective interpersonal skills.

Action-centred leadership (E: 8 pp 208-209; F: 8 pp 182-183; G: 11 pp 288-290)

John Adair (4) argues that to be effective, a leader has to combine three functions:
- *Task functions.* These are the objectives of the group and involve the planning of activities and the allocation of resources.
- *Team functions.* The leader must demonstrate concern for the well-being and morale of the group to ensure effective performance.
- *Individual functions.* As well as meeting team needs, it is important to satisfy the needs of individuals by giving encouragement and providing development opportunities.

Further, to succeed, Adair believes that all three functions need to be fulfilled. In essence, he views the leader as a person who can establish and strengthen unity of purpose through the efforts of individuals:

"In industry, as in every other sphere where free and able people need to co-operate, effective leadership is founded upon respect and trust, not fear and submission. Respect and trust help to inspire whole-hearted commitment in a team; fear and submission merely produce compliance. Leadership involves focusing the efforts of a group towards a common goal and enabling them to work together as a team. A leader should be directive in a democratic way".
(5)

The contingency approach (D: 8 pp 123-124; E: 8 p 210; G: 11 pp 296-299)

Contingency theories are based on the belief that leadership styles can and should vary according to the situation. Further, that different people can take on leadership roles according to the prevailing situation and circumstances. Fiedler's (6) contingency model seeks to depict a leader's ability to exercise influence over a group by using an appropriate leadership style. According to Fiedler, the extent to which this is successfully accomplished depends on three 'critical dimensions':
- *Position power.* The formal power which the organization has given the leader.
- *Task structure.* The extent to which tasks can be clearly defined and explained to staff.
- *Leader-group relations.* The degree to which a team like, and trust a leader and are willing to support him or her.

Fiedler's concludes that a 'favourable' situation is more likely to arise if: (a) the leader has formal power and authority and (b) the tasks are clear and the leader is respected by the group. An 'unfavourable' situation occurs when the opposite conditions arise. The most appropriate strategy for the leader in both favourable and unfavourable situations is to be directive and task orientated. If the situation is moderately favourable or unfavourable, the leader should adopt a more supportive approach.

The managerial grid (D: 8: pp 122-123; E: 8 pp 211-213; G: 5 pp 117-119)

Blake and Mouton's (7) concept of leadership is based on a balance between 'concern for production' and 'concern for people'. Concern for production includes the attitudes of supervisors towards work systems and productivity levels. Concern for people includes the development of effective working relationships and personal commitment. They identify a range of leadership styles between these two dimensions. For example, the approach which shows little concern for people or for production is referred as a 'impoverished management'. Blake and Mouton's 'managerial grid' can be used as a practical tool for identifying leadership positions and after this, appropriate training and development can assist in reinforcing an optimum leadership style.

The managerial grid also provides a framework for self-assessment so that managers can assess their own leadership styles. The most effective style is considered to be 'team management'. This style is particularly appropriate for hospitality and tourism organizations where production and people skills are fully integrated.

The continuum theory (E: 8 pp 213-214;
F: 8 pp 184-185; G: 11 pp 294- 295)
Tannenbaum and Schmidt (8) offer a leadership
model which presents a continuum of possible
behaviours, ranging from authoritarian to
democratic. To identify an individual manager's style
on this continuum, typical behaviours are considered
in relation to the preferred level of supervision and
control of staff. This approach reveals four main
styles of leadership:
- *Tells*. The leader informs the group of the action
  they must take, without any prior discussion.
- *Sells*. The leader is sensitive to the fact staff may
  resist decisions which are mainly imposed and
  so attempts to persuade staff to accept particular
  courses of action either before or after decisions
  are taken.
- *Consults*. The leader listens to the views of staff
  before making most decisions.
- *Joins*. Problems are defined by the leader and
  boundaries established within which the group
  makes a decision.

Tannenbaum and Schmidt suggest that three forces
affect the adoption of a given leadership style.
Further, that effective leaders are aware of these
forces and behave appropriately in terms of
understanding themselves, other individuals, the
group as a whole and the situation in which they
work. The three forces are:
- *Forces in the manager*. These include the
  background and experience of the individual,
  their personality, value system and confidence in
  their staff.
- *Forces in the subordinate*. These include the
  need for independence and willingness to accept
  responsibility as well as experience and
  knowledge.
- *Forces in the situation*. The characteristics of the
  situation encompass the culture of the
  organization, pressure of time and the type of
  problem to be solved.

Likert
(D: 8 pp 124-125; E: 8 p 211; G: 7 pp 185-186)
Renis Likert (9) classifies leadership styles under
four broad headings:
- *Autocratic*. The leader makes all the decisions
  for the group and instructs them - often without
  showing concern for the feelings of individual
  members.
- *Persuasive*. The leader makes all the decisions,
  but he or she makes an effort to sell ideas to the
  group rather than impose them. If the group
  rejects a particular idea, the leader may still
  implement the decision if it is considered to be a
  necessary step.

- *Consultative*. The leader discusses the issues
  relating to a particular decision with the group
  prior to making a decision. The final course of
  action taken may or may not be influenced by
  the views of the group.
- *Democratic*. The leader provides an opportunity
  for staff to participate in the decision-making
  process and accepts their conclusions.

Selecting a leadership style (D: 8 pp 125-127; E: 8
pp 214-215; F: 8 p 186; G: 11 pp 302-303)
There is no simple answer to the question 'which is
the best style of leadership?' Different situations
demand different leadership styles. For example, a
hotel manager dealing with an emergency situation,
such as a fire, may not have sufficient time to consult
with members of staff before taking decisions.
However, the same leader should ideally use
different styles in differing situations and
circumstances. A willingness to adopt a flexible
approach thereby takes into account the attitudes of
group members, their needs and their current
situation. Further, it is also likely that different types
of leader will be required at the various stages of an
organization's development.

A number of studies on leadership in the hospitality
industry have been undertaken but they offer
different conclusions. Keegan (1) argues the case for
a supportive, behavioural approach to leadership:

*"The challenge for us is not so much to change the
job, but to provide the managerial leadership that
would create an environment in which the employee's
real needs are satisfied. Such a leadership is
characterized as being personal, supportive and
participative, and is firmly based on a solid
relationship between the manager and the
employees. This managerial leadership should be an
integral part of the hospitality environment, a
behavioural model as it were, how best to behave
with people in general whether they be guests or
employees. Such a leadership style is, in many ways
in direct opposition to the leadership traditionally
associated with our industry. We must change and
change dramatically, so let our goal be then to
develop this new leadership for our industry."*

Although Keegan favours a people-oriented
approach, as was stated earlier, it is difficult to be
definitive on this topic as there numerous factors to
take into account prior to adopting a particular
leadership style. These include:
- The nature of the organization and its culture.
- The characteristics of the manager e.g.
  personality and attitude.
- The characteristics of the staff e.g. commitment
  and confidence.

- The basis of the leadership position e.g. expert power.
- The type of decisions that have to be made.
- The type of work to be undertaken e.g. routine and well structured.
- The influence of the external environment.

Ultimately, the most effective leader is one who takes account of all the variables and maintains a flexible approach to their role.

CONCLUSION

The role of the leader continually changes according to the situation and the people involved. It is difficult therefore, to identify a set of skills that will guarantee effective leadership. The extent to which good leaders are born or made has been the subject of debate for many years and today the general opinion is that leadership skills can be learnt. Leadership styles have been analyzed by different management writers and these range from the action-centred approach proposed by Adair to continuum theory developed by Tannenbaum and Schmidt. In selecting an appropriate leadership style flexibility is the key to success so as to take into account the many variables which influence the behaviour of people in organizations.

References:

1. B.M.Keegan. 'Leadership in the Hospitality Industry' in E. Casse and R. Reuland (eds). *The Management of Hospitality*. Pergamon, Oxford, 1983 p 78.
2. J.R.P. French and B. Rowen. 'The Basis of Social Power' in D. Cartwright and A.F. Zander (eds), *Group Dynamics: Research and Theory*. Harper and Row, London, 1968.
3. R. G. Walker. 'Wellsprings of Managerial Leadership' *Cornell HRA Quarterly*, Vol. 27, No. 2, August 1986, pp 14-16.
4. J. Adair. *Action Centred Leadership*. Gower, London, 1979.
5. J. Adair. *Effective Teambuilding*. Gower, London 1986.
6. F.E. Fiedler. *A Theory of Leadership Effectiveness*. McGraw-Hill, New York, 1967.
7. R.R. Blake and J.S. Mouton. *The Managerial Grid*. Gulf, Houston, TX: 1964.
8. R. Tannenbaum and W.H. Schmidt. 'How to Choose a Leadership Pattern'. *Harvard Business Review*, May-June, 1973, pp 162-180.
9. R. Likert. *The Human Organization*, McGraw-Hill, New York, 1967.

Review questions:

1. Select a hospitality or tourism organization with which you are familiar and study the behaviour of two leaders. Compare and contrast the two different leadership styles and suggest the steps which could be taken to improve the effectiveness of the individuals concerned.

2. Discuss what you believe to be the most important characteristics of an effective leader in a hospitality or tourism organization.

3. Discuss the advantages and disadvantages of allowing staff to participate in decision-making.

EXTENSION

Read: Chapter 7 of *Hospitality Management: A Human Resources Approach* (G: 7 pp 171-196).

This chapter concentrates on the process of management and covers issues such as delegation, authority and responsibility.

Extension questions:

1. Explain the need for management control in the hospitality and tourism industries. Discuss how a manager can balance the benefits of delegation with the need to maintain control of staff.

2. Compare and contrast employee-centred and job-centred styles of supervision.

3. Discuss the strategy you would adopt to implement a behavioural approach to control in a hospitality or tourism organization.

Practical exercises:

1. Read the case study in E: 8 on page 217 (A8.4) and answer the questions.

2. Assess yourself as a leader and identify the qualities you possess. Discuss your views with a colleague. To what extent do your findings agree?

3. Prepare a ten minute presentation on 'Tomorrow's leaders in the hospitality and tourism industries - what will be required?'

10
TIME MANAGEMENT

INTRODUCTION

"I suppose the most essential part of this struggle is the management of one's time, and here there are a number of key things that can be done. I have always believed that when I am at work I should work as hard and effectively as I can, all the time that I am there, but that equally, when I am not working, there should be a clear line between the two experiences. In order to cover the sheer amounts of work, of contact, reading and writing and so on, it really is necessary to use every moment of enforced working time to the best effect."
J. Harvey Jones, *Making It Happen*, Fontana, 1988.

Managers in the hospitality and tourism industries are faced with the challenge of dealing with a wide variety of tasks from organizing staff and controlling costs to liaising with customers. The way managers organize their time is critical if they are to be effective. In order to improve time management skills individuals need to understand the problems that can result if these skills are not developed and to learn techniques which can help them with their daily workloads.

The purpose of this chapter is to consider why time is such a valuable resource and to highlight the main symptoms of poor time management skills. Following on from this attention is given to describing the techniques which can be used to improve the way time is managed together with the approach which should be taken for general management tasks.

In this chapter:
- The significance of time
  (E: 32 p 583; F: 6 pp 138-139)
- Symptoms of poor time management
  (E: 32 pp 583-584; F: 6 pp 140-142)
- Behaviour patterns (F: 6 pp 140-142)
- Prioritizing (E: 32 p 588)
- Adopting time management techniques (E: 32 pp 588-592; F: 6 pp 140-144; pp 148-149)
- Dealing with tasks (F: 6 pp 145-149)
- Evaluation (E: 32 pp 587-588; p 590; p 592)

REVIEW

The significance of time
(E: 32 p 583; F: 6 pp 138-139)
Time is one of the four characteristics of the universe (after length, breadth and height). Time only travels one way and any given time only comes once. Time is a valuable resource for both individuals and organizations because it cannot be stored and the amount available is limited. For the world of business, time represents money and it is therefore measured and recorded very carefully by employers. For example an accountant or solicitor will charge fees which are based on hourly rates.

Time management is in essence concerned with planning and being in control. Without adequate planning crises often occur and as a result more time is invested in resolving the problems. The objective of time management, therefore, is to make the best use of a valuable resource.

Symptoms of poor time management
(E: 32 pp 583-584; F: 6 pp 140-142)
The first step towards improving the way time is managed is the identification of symptoms. For managers in the hospitality and tourism industries the nature of the work usually involves long hours and shifts with little time to relax or reflect on how efficient they are in the use of their time. It is important, therefore, that managers are able to identify signs that they are not managing their time effectively. The following are possible consequences of poor time management:

- *Too much to do.* A classic problem, often linked to the manager working long hours. In essence the manager is no longer in control and as a result tasks are not completed and crises occur more frequently.

- *No time for planning.* A situation which arises when managers are compelled to spend all their time in dealing with the present and consequently time for forward planning and development of the organization and its human resources is restricted. According to Handy (1) the manager is responsible for the future.

- *Reacting to events.* A further indicator that managers are not in control but are 'fire-fighting'.

- *Resolving problems for subordinates.* The need to mediate or intervene in problem-solving which is indirectly related to key priorities may mean that managers have less time for their own tasks.

- *Stress.* A possible consequence of poor time management, stress can manifest itself in many ways from absence to difficulties with interpersonal relationships.

- *Being less effective at work.* This can lead to the creation of a poor impression with senior management and in turn, may impede promotional prospects.

- *Activity mania.* If there is no detailed plan of the tasks to be completed, jobs may be left incomplete and managers may find themselves rushing from one problem to another. There is no time for thinking and the law of diminishing returns begins to operate.

- *Less leisure time.* As more time is being spent at work, interpersonal relationships at home start to become threatened.

Behaviour patterns (F: 6 pp 140-142)

Research has revealed that particular types of people are more likely to have poor time management skills. These include individuals who are trying to attract recognition by taking on too much work and those who are too organized and spend all their time planning tasks. Others include those who are afraid of making mistakes and those resentful towards the organization. Examples of these behaviours are as follows:

- *Recognition seeking.* Some individuals are keen to let others know how much work they do. They therefore demonstrate this by physically rushing around. They have problems in meeting deadlines and others comment that they take too much on.

- *Over-organized.* Over planning and listing of tasks to be completed can in itself be very time consuming. This stops the individual actually undertaking the tasks.

- *Fear of making mistakes.* In order to avoid making any errors some people spend a good deal of time thoroughly researching all the consequences and implications of taking any action.

- *Resentful of the organization.* Some individuals may be unhappy with the way the organization has treated them. For example they may have been turned down for promotion in the past. Due to their disillusionment with the organization it is likely that such an individual will be reluctant to take forward the organizations' objectives.

Prioritizing (E: 32 p 588)

There are a number of approaches that can be used to identify the order in which tasks should be dealt with. For example it should be possible to distinguish between long-term priorities (LTPs) and short-term priorities (STPs). Usually LTPs are associated with organizations and the establishment of aims and objectives. For the individual manager a LTP maybe acquiring a particular qualification which would increase their chances of promotion.

Adopting time management techniques

(E: 32 pp 588-592; F: 6 pp 140-144, pp 148-149)
Different techniques are available to assist individuals in using their time more efficiently. These include:

- *Using planning aids.* Diaries, work-planners and daily schedule forms are the tools which are most frequently used. Another technique is based on the 'MOP', or the 'must, ought and prefer' principle and involves categorizing tasks under one of the three headings. Individuals often spend much of their time on preferred tasks, avoiding the 'must' and 'ought' work. One consequence of listing all the tasks that need to be undertaken is that action is usually required to cope with the demands. This may result in delegation or the elimination of some tasks from the list. The urgent versus important matrix (E: 32 p 590) is another technique which can be used by managers to help them choose between undertaking tasks which are critical to the business in the immediate future and those which are significant in the longer term.

- *Allocating time for yourself.* It is important that time is set aside each day for the manager when they know they will not be committed to any particular activities.

- *Delegation.* Managers cannot deal with every task and it is important that they learn when and how to delegate successfully. Questions that individuals need to ask themselves centre on whether or not anyone else in the organization could deal with the particular task.

- *Self-motivation.* In order to achieve the aim of managing time effectively it is important to reward any success in this area.

- *Avoid leaving tasks.* Sometimes individuals avoid particular tasks because they feel ill-equipped to deal with them. It is important that the underlying reasons for the avoidance are identified and action is taken.

  For example a hospitality manager may have a fear of using a computer because they feel they have not acquired the necessary skills to operate the technology. Such problems need to be faced and overcome.

- *Use of slack time.* There are many occasions during the course of a working week when spare time becomes available. This often occurs when individuals are travelling on trains or waiting for an appointment. In order to avoid wasting time managers need to have work with them that they can use the time to do. For example reading documents or drafting letters.

- *Time dualling.* With careful planning, it is sometimes possible to complete two tasks at one time. This is also known as poly phasing.

Dealing with tasks (F: 6 pp 145-149)
A significant proportion of the work undertaken by hospitality and tourism managers is of an administrative nature. By focusing on how these tasks are approached it is possible to find ways of reducing the time spent on them. The key areas where improvements can usually be made are:

- *Reading documents.* Managers deal with a wide range of paperwork - from memos and letters to reports. There is not usually enough time to read every word in a letter or report and it becomes necessary to scan documents and identify key points. Undertaking a speed-reading course can help managers to improve their skills in this area.

- *Responding to paperwork.* In order to minimize the time spent dealing with paperwork managers need to decide quickly whether or not they need to follow-up, forward, file or forget the item.

- *Managing meetings.* A lot of time can be wasted due to poor management of meetings. In order to ensure meetings are effective a number of questions need to be addressed. These include whether the meeting is really necessary, the aims and the amount of time actually required.

- *Handling interruptions.* During the course of a working day managers will experience a number of interruptions to their work. In order to deal with these interruptions positively it is important that individuals learn how to control the situation. For example giving people a clear indication of how much time can be allocated to a particular discussion.

- *Using the telephone.* The telephone is frequently used by managers. They should set aside a period to make the calls and plan what is to be said. In order to avoid answering phone calls continually, managers should field the calls to their assistant or subordinate.

- *Routine paperwork.* Given the nature of managerial work a significant proportion of the tasks are routine and repetitive. In order to reduce the time taken to deal with these tasks individuals should set aside a period of time to deal with routine matters as quickly as possible.

- *Prioritizing tasks.* The development of systems which deal with regular tasks effectively and speedily should be encouraged. This will allow more free time and decrease stress. Systems can be developed by: (a) setting aside periods of time for routine tasks each day; (b) keeping a diary and task schedule and (c) allowing sufficient time and space to respond to non-routine work tasks.

Evaluation (E: 32 pp 587-588; p 590; p 592)
In attempting to improve time management skills it is beneficial to review past events and undertake a process of evaluation. The steps that can be taken include:

- *Costing time.* By calculating how much an hour a managers' time costs the importance of managing time effectively becomes clear. There are different ways in which this can be achieved such as identifying significant job elements (SJEs) (E: 32 p 587).

- *Review each day.* By reflecting on work undertaken it is possible to evaluate how successful the day has been and to identify tasks which need to be carried forward.

- *Analyzing problems.* In order to avoid crises recurring again it is important to analyze them and learn from them.

CONCLUSION

Time is as important as money to organizations and yet it is not always treated with the same respect. There are a number of examples of the consequences of poor time management, from reactive rather than pro-active strategies to individuals suffering from overwork and stress.

The key to managing time more effectively is using techniques which allow the individual to be in control of their working day. As hospitality and tourism managers cope with increasingly demanding jobs it is vital that they look closely at the way in which they approach their jobs and adopt new techniques which assist them to achieve their goals and objectives.

Reference:

1. C.B. Handy, *Understanding Organizations*. Penguin Books, London, 1985.

Review questions:

1. Discuss the importance of managers who use their time effectively for hospitality and tourism organizations.

2. Identify the difficulties that senior management may experience in requesting staff to review the way they spend their time at work.

3. To what extent does the leadership style of the hospitality or tourism manager influence the way they use their time at work?

EXTENSION

Read: Chapter 4 of *Hospitality Management: A Human Resources Approach* (G: 4 pp 86-113)

This chapter focuses upon the work that hospitality managers do. The first part concentrates on the nature and process of management. The discussion then moves forward to review studies that have been undertaken to determine how much time hospitality managers assign to different roles and concludes with a section on the measurement of managerial effectiveness.

Extension questions:

1. Discuss the extent to which hospitality and tourism managers spend their time differently compared with managers in other industries.

2. Identify the criteria that could be used to evaluate how effective managers in the hospitality and tourism industries are in managing their time.

3. Mintzberg describes the manager's job in terms of various 'roles'. Which roles are most relevant to hospitality and tourism managers and why?

Practical exercises:

1. Assess your own time management behaviour by answering the question in E: 32 pp 586-587.

2. Over a period of three weeks conduct an analysis of how you spend your time studying. To complete this analysis you will first need to draw up a list of your key activities. These will include, for example, attending lectures and tutorials, making notes, preparing assignments, reading and researching in the library.

    In designing your time log you will need to develop a set of symbols which will indicate whether an activity was self-initiated, who was involved in the activity and how much time was used.

    Once the data has been collected you need to analyze the material and establish how much time you spent on particular activities, the proportion of these activities that involved other people and were self-initiated. Having produced your findings identify ways in which your use of time could be improved.

2. Arrange to 'shadow' a manager in a hospitality or tourism organization for a day and record how they spend their time. Prepare a short report reviewing the time management skills of the manager.

3. Prepare a ten minute presentation for senior managers on 'How the hospitality/tourism manager will spend their time in the year 2010'.

11
DECISION-MAKING

INTRODUCTION

"If I had to sum up in one word the qualities that make a good manager, I'd say it all comes down to decisiveness. You can use the fanciest computers in the world and you can gather all the charts and numbers, but in the end you have to bring all your information together, set up a time-table, and act." Lee Iacocca (cited in F: 5 p 100).

A key part of a manager's job is concerned with making decisions. These range from long-term impacts on the organization such as moving into new markets, to those which are more immediate like reducing prices. A manager making a decision needs to consider both quality and acceptability. The quality of the decision concerns the extent to which the solution must be accurate and correct e.g. a surgeon performing an operation. It is also important to consider the acceptability of the solution to the people who will be affected by it e.g. the selection of staff uniforms.

The style of decision-making that a manager adopts is dependent on a range of factors including the politics of the organization and personal characteristics. Rational decision-making consists of a number of steps and non-routine decisions need particular attention. In order to improve the quality of decision-making managers need to allow enough time to consider all the issues involved.

In this chapter:
- Types of decision
  (E: 6 p 155; F: 5 pp 105-106; G: 4 pp 94-95)
- Decision-making styles
  (A: 10 pp 155-157; F: 5 pp 110-111)
- Rational decision-making (A: 10 pp 158-167)
- Dealing with non-routine decisions
  (F: 5 pp 107-122)
- Improving the quality of decision making
  (A: 10 pp 167-176)

REVIEW

Types of decision
(E: 6 p 155; F: 5 pp 105-106; G: 4 pp 94-95)
Mintzberg classifies the essential functions of a manager into three main groups, one of which concerns decision-making.

Managers have an entrepreneurial role where they take decisions which are concerned with initiating and planning changes. For example the accommodation manager of a student hall of residence may decide to contract out the laundry service. Likewise when unexpected events occur such as the breakdown of the central heating system in a hotel the manager has to make the best decision possible in the circumstances. Managers also have to make difficult decisions with regard to the allocation of resources such as finance and staff e.g. reducing budget allocations. In addition, managers are often involved in negotiating with others such as suppliers.

As well as classifying decisions according to the management role, they can also be analyzed in terms of the frequency with which they occur. Routine decisions are predictable and usually procedures are established for individuals in the organization to follow. Crisis decisions are caused by an emergency and some organizations are more prepared than others to cope with such situations. Non-routine decisions are often challenging but not crisis driven. Individuals often need to be creative to deal with decisions of this nature.

Decision-making styles
(A: 10 pp 155-157; F: 5 pp 110-111)
Managers in different settings may arrive at different decisions when confronted by the same situation. The style that individual managers adopt when making a decision is influenced by a number of factors. These include:

- Past experience and the success they have achieved.
- Habit - managers are often reluctant to change their approach.
- The politics of the organization and the way the company expects managers to operate as well as the need to appease certain powerful individuals in the organization.
- The importance of the decision and the extent to which careful consideration is required.
- An unwillingness to seek help where the manager feels this would be a poor reflection on his/her abilities.
- Expectations of others in the organization and the need to fit this image.
- The level of information and time available to make the decision, which may need to be carefully balanced.
- The extent to which decisions are successful or correct.

Individuals invariably make different decisions drawing upon prior experience and decision-making guidelines and rules.

Further, the style can change if decisions are made as part of a group. The six main styles are:

- *Feelings based.* The emphasis is on what the individual feels is the best solution and is based on preferences and inner values.
- *Hyper-vigilant.* Making the decision can lead to the creation of anxiety and as a result, the efficiency of the decision-making process decreases. Becoming too concerned with the details can lead to a loss of perspective and lack of clarity.
- *Avoidant.* Ignoring problems or engaging in delaying tactics. In essence seeking short-term comfort regardless of long-term costs.
- *Impulsive.* Making decisions rapidly and acting on initial reactions.
- *Compliant.* Individuals conform to what others expect of them and follow their signals. The decision is influenced or made by others.
- *Ethical.* The decision is based on ethics e.g. religious beliefs.

Joint decision-making can take three different forms:

- *Competitive.* The decision is concerned with scarce resources and as a result there has to be a winner and a loser. The individual who adopts a competitive style is determined to be a winner.
- *Compliant.* The manager is unassertive and goes along with the decision being made by others.
- *Collaborative.* The group works together for a decision which is satisfactory to all members.

Rational decision-making (A: 10 pp 158-167). Rational decision-making is another style which consists of two stages. The first stage involves confronting and making the decision and the second is concerned with implementation and evaluation. In order to make a successful decision it is necessary to have an open mind to the information available and to develop as many options as possible. The seven steps in the rational decision-making process are as follows:

Stage One:
(a) Confronting
Facing a decision involves considering all available information. It is usually the information which encourages an individual to make a decision. For example a personnel manager after reading a research report on strategies for reducing labour turnover in the hospitality and tourism industries, may decide to introduce a job-share scheme and a creche into her hotel to attract women returners. As well as reacting to external information individuals also need to be aware of their inner feelings, for example a successful manager may at the mid-point

of her career, decide that she is more interested in the quality of life and decide to start her own business. When confronting a decision it is important to develop a clear focus and be fully aware of the implications e.g. moving to work for a new company.

(b) Generating options and gathering information
Decisions do not always involve straightforward choices. Developing options is a creative process which can be assisted by using techniques such as brainstorming. Good decisions are only made when good information is available. Whilst the aim should be to gather as much information as possible, it is important to know when to stop so as to avoid being overloaded with material.

(c) Assessing the effects of options
Psychologists Irving Janis and Leon Mann (1) have put forward a balance sheet approach for assessing the consequences of decisions. Their procedure involves taking into account a series of considerations in four areas: (a) gains and losses for self; (b) gains and losses for others; (c) self-approval or self-disapproval and (d) approval or disapproval from others. The consequences which need to be taken into consideration will vary with the type of decision being made. For example if an individual is changing their job they need to consider the change of location, travel time, level of work, security, environment and status.

(d) Commitment
Making a decision is one step but being committed to it is another. Commitment usually requires a high degree of personal effort and hard work. Sometimes decisions are finely balanced and there may be regrets about the action which has to be taken.

(e) Planning
The skills of planning include setting clear objectives, which are realistic, precise and give a time span for achievement. It is sometimes helpful to develop sub-objectives so that the task does not appear too daunting. At this stage it is also important to identify any difficulties and where necessary seek assistance and support. Preparing the plan in writing helps to clarify the process and acts as a basis for monitoring performance.

Stage Two:
(f) Implementation
Once the decision reaches the implementation phase it is essential to take into consideration timing, post-decisional conflicts, feedback and guilt. A caterer responsible for the introduction of a new self-service restaurant will need to ensure that the change is introduced at the right time of the year and be

prepared to cope with the compromises which are being made e.g. not investing in new kitchen equipment. The catering manager should encourage feedback from customers and staff and will need to establish a system for judging the feedback. It is important that the feedback is analyzed carefully and that where appropriate it is acted upon. The catering manager may experience feelings of guilt if inwardly he considers the finance invested in the new service system should really have been spent on new staff changing rooms, for example.

(g) Review

Finally it is important to review the consequences of attaining or not attaining the goals which have been set. Where a decision does not work it should be abandoned and a new decision taken.

Dealing with non-routine decisions
(F: 5 pp 107-122).

Non-routine decisions require time and much thought. The process involves consideration, consultation, appraising, communicating and checking. The degree of consultation undertaken will be dependent on the management style. For example the manager of a travel agency may be totally autocratic always issuing instructions to her staff and never encouraging their views or ideas. The level of consultation will also be linked to the size and ownership of the organization. In a large international hotel company most of the decision-making will be undertaken by a head office team.

Vroom and Yetton (2) developed a series of rules to guide the extent to which managers should involve others in the decision process. It should be noted that it may be necessary to involve particular individuals in the decision-making process because they possess unique skills and knowledge. For example the general manager of a hotel may wish to install a computerized reservations system and should therefore identify any individuals in the organization who have the expertise to help her make the decision regarding which system to purchase. When consulting with others it is important to consider the time that this process takes, the cost and the degree to which the discussions should be kept confidential.

Choosing between a range of alternatives is an important step in the decision making process. The simplest approach is to list the advantages and disadvantages of each alternative. A more refined approach is to consider essential, desirable and unacceptable characteristics of a solution. For example a personnel manager establishing the person specification for a room attendant will be able to identify the essential and desirable selection criteria. This process can be added to by using a form of

weighting for the criteria. For example, experience of working in a first class hotel may be given a rating of five points because it is considered to be an essential requirement. Other techniques which can be used include decision trees and risk preference.

Once the decision has been taken it is important to select the most appropriate channel of communication and to monitor and review the success or otherwise of the action taken.

Improving the quality of decision-making
(A: 10 pp 167-176).

Decisions often involve anxiety because risks are being taken. In addition decisions are not always straight forward and a complex range of issues have to be considered. In order to improve the quality of the process managers need to ensure they have sufficient time to reach the correct decision by gathering information and listening to inner feelings. In order to be in touch with inner feelings the following steps should be taken:

- *Taking time.* Before making an important decision an individual should allow themselves sufficient time to consider all the issues involved.

- *Collecting information.* As information is gathered it is usually easier to reach a decision e.g. a hotel manager considering building an extension to provide an extra ten guest bedrooms.

- *Managing anxiety.* It is important that the individual learns how to cope with their own anxiety to avoid the negative effects this can have on the decision-making process.

It is also important that they avoid putting too much pressure on themselves to make the right decision. Analyzing self-perceptions and the perception of others is an integral part of the decision making process. Clarifying goals and being realistic is also essential.

For example an entrepreneur may be considering moving into the catering industry and buying a restaurant. Before he decides to purchase a particular property he should spend time undertaking a thorough market feasibility study to obtain the necessary information about the viability of the business. The individual should also consider how he really feels about managing his own business and whether or not he has the character to become a successful restaurateur.

CONCLUSION

Making decisions is an everyday activity for managers in the hospitality and tourism industries. Decisions often involve the allocation of resources and the development of the business and it is therefore essential that managers learn to approach the decision-making process in a logical way using the techniques available to reduce the risks of taking the wrong action.

The style of decision-making that an individual adopts will depend on their previous experience. For example a marketing manager in the tourism industry involved in launching a new product will base her decisions on a number of factors including the success she has achieved in the past and the expectations of her senior managers. The style used will be one of six types from feelings-based to avoidant. Rational decision-making is a process involving a number of steps which should be taken carefully and not rushed. When non-routine decisions have to be made, particular attention should be given to appraising the different courses of action available.

References:

1.   I. Jarvis and L. Mann, *Decision Making: A Psychological Analysis of Conflict Choice and Commitment.* The Free Press, New York, 1977.
2.   V.H. Vroom and P.W. Yetton, *Leadership and Decision-Making.* The Pittsburgh Press, 1973.

Review questions:

1.   From your experience of a hospitality or tourism organization identify a significant decision which was made by management. Discuss the steps which were taken before the decision was made and outline how the process could have been improved.

2.   Review the decision-making styles of three managers in a hospitality or tourism organization and comment on the strengths and weaknesses of each approach.

3.   Discuss the extent to which managers should be the main decision-makers in an organization.

EXTENSION

Read: Chapter 3 of *Hospitality Management: A Human Resources Approach* (G: 3 pp 52-85)

The chapter reviews the importance of organization structure and the different approaches e.g. bureaucracy and human relations. In the first part of the chapter the purpose of an organization structure is explained and this is followed by an analysis of the different approaches and their relevance to the hospitality industry. The arguments for and against centralization and decentralization are presented and organizational relationships are explored.

Extension questions:

1.   Compare and contrast the styles of decision-making which are likely to exist in a bureaucratic and scientific organization structure.

2.   Explain the main factors which should be considered when designing an organization structure to ensure effective decision-making.

3.   Discuss how organizational relationships can influence decision-making styles.

Practical exercises:

1.   Select a decision you are currently involved in making. Identify the options from which you can make your decision. Prepare a balance sheet for assessing the consequences of each option. In what ways has this process changed your approach to the decision? (A: 10 p 162).

2.   With reference to a hospitality or tourism organization with which you are familiar identify a decision you would like to see implemented. Prepare a realistic plan for the implementation phase and discuss any problems you foresee.

3.   Prepare a report for senior management outlining the benefits and disbenefits of group decision-making.

12
PROBLEM-SOLVING

INTRODUCTION

Managers in the hospitality and tourism industries regularly encounter a number of problems in the course of their work. These problems may be concerned with customers and their demands, staff, suppliers or competitors. Given the wide range of problems which can occur it is important that managers develop a rational approach to finding solutions. It should be appreciated that problem-solving and decision-making are closely related and that the material covered in Chapter 11 is very relevant to this chapter. Most decisions are made to solve problems and most problems have a number of possible solutions - a decision has to be taken as to which one to adopt. For example a reservations manager may be trying to increase the occupancy level of his hotel. To achieve this aim he can either offer the rooms at a reduced tariff, offer a free bottle of champagne to any guest staying more than three nights or include dinner in the charge for the room. From these three solutions the reservations manager will have to make a decision.

In this chapter:
- Categorizing problems (F: 4 pp 66-70)
- Individual approaches to problems (A: 11 p 179)
- Accepting a problem (A: 11 p 184)
- Defining the problem (A: 11 pp 184-189; D: 8 pp 128-129; E: 6 p 156; F: 4 p 92)
- Collecting information (D: 8 p 129; E: 6 p 156)
- Developing solutions (D: 8 pp 129-130; E: 6 p 157; F: 4 pp 70-99)
- Selecting, implementing and evaluating a solution (A: 11 pp 190-192; D: 8 pp 131-132; E: 6 pp 157-158)

REVIEW

Categorizing problems (F: 4 pp 66-70)
In order to develop a successful solution to a problem it is necessary to understand its nature and complexity. Tudor Rickards (1) has developed five different classifications for problems. The first type of problem has only one correct answer e.g. calculating the number of meals that a restaurant needs to serve to achieve break-even point.

The second type of problem requires a certain level of creative thought for a solution to be found e.g. a chef who has to serve a business lunch for a group of thirty people when only twenty-two people had been expected.

For some problems, it is important that solutions are tried and tested before they are implemented. For example the development of new recipes will involve an element of trial and error before the final product is approved. There will be occasions when a problem may appear to have a straightforward answer but is complicated by the human element e.g. the general manager of a hotel may wish to restructure the organization. Whilst on paper such an exercise may be easy to undertake, when the plan is implemented, and the issue of redundancies is raised, the answer may not appear to be so simple.

Another approach to assessing a problem is to consider its position on a spectrum ranging from 'straightforward' to 'complex'. In the former situation knowledge and skills are available to develop a solution. With complex problems, however, there are a number of issues involved and as a result there is not an easy answer e.g. increasing the number of tourists to a particular destination may involve considerable investment in new facilities and transport systems.

Problems can also be viewed in terms of their technical demands and the need for professional expertise. For example a leisure centre manager will need the help of a specialist to resolve problems with the water system in the pool. In some circumstances problems have a high emotional impact and a personnel manager, may, for example have to deal with staff who are upset with their working conditions.

It is important, that problems are examined carefully before any steps are taken to develop solutions. By producing a matrix it may be easier to understand the nature of the problem (p 69).

Individual approaches to problems (A: 11 p 179)
Whilst individuals will deal with different problems in a variety of ways everyone has a particular style of managing problems. Initially the reaction may be to try and avoid the problem by taking some form of alternative action e.g. cancelling a meeting to discuss budgets because the necessary data has not been gathered. Alternatively a manager may try to provide immediate solutions without giving sufficient thought to the issues involved and the implications of the quick action.

Another approach is for the individual to immerse themselves in the detail of the problem with the result that they do not have a clear overview of the situation and cannot develop a satisfactory solution. In order to manage the problem there may be occasions when a manager takes the easy way out of a difficult situation and complies with the wishes of others. Finally, a small proportion of managers will possess a natural ability to deal with problems in an entirely rational way.

Accepting a problem (A: 11 p 184)

The first step towards overcoming a problem is accepting that it exists. The extent to which people accept problems depends on their attitude. For example a hospitality manager who considers problem-solving to be an inherent part of their work will not try to avoid difficulties. Taking responsibility for problems requires courage but it is a very positive action which will assist the development of solutions. As well as recognizing that a problem exists, time needs to be allocated to resolving the difficulties.

Defining the problem (A: 11 pp 184-189; D: 8 pp 128-129; E: 6 p 156; F: 4 p 92)

Having identified that a problem exists it is important to develop a full understanding of the issues involved. For example a hospitality manager receiving a high level of customer complaints needs to determine how serious the problems is. This may involve talking to members of staff to gain their views and generating explanations.

Diagrams can help to understand the problem. The 'fishbone diagram' is one example and 'force field analysis' is another approach which identifies opposing pressures in a particular situation. For example a hotel experiencing a high level of customer complaints may be able to identify factors which have promoted the situation and factors which could lead to a decrease in the number of complaints.

Distinguishing between cause and effect is an important stage in the problem definition process. Once the root causes of the problem have been clearly identified the next step involves the establishment of objectives and the identification of the people involved in the process and the implications of the solutions for them.

Collecting information (D: 8 p 129; E: 6 p 156)

In order to make a correct decision it is necessary to gather as much relevant information as possible before any action is taken. For example if there is a high labour turnover problem, information could be collected from analyzing personnel records, conducting exit interviews and circulating

questionnaires. The information gathered should be examined to establish its accuracy, validity and reliability.

Developing solutions

(D: 8 pp 129-130; E: 6 p 157; F: 4 pp 70-99)
Generating possible solutions to a problem can be approached in an analytical or a creative way. Analytical thought relies on logic and seeks to narrow down the range of possible solutions whereas creative thought aims to open up the range of answers. Edward de Bono developed the concept of lateral thinking and he compared it with vertical (analytical) thinking. Lateral thinking uses information to stimulate new ideas, looks for differences and encourages distraction. In contrast vertical thinking seeks positive or negative answers, concentrates on only relevant factors and follows an expected path.

There are a range of techniques which can be used to encourage lateral thinking. These include:

- *Awareness*. Being aware of current ideas.
- *Dominant Ideas*. Such ideas affect the way a problem is viewed. For example employees in the hospitality and tourism industries will have different attitudes to the role of trade unions but these will be shaped by the dominant ideas about trade unions in society.
- *Assumptions*. Sometimes individuals have assumptions about problems. An example given by Edward de Bono is that people expect to pay less per hour for their car to be parked for a long time. Another way of looking at this problem is that the longer cars are parked the more congestion builds up. The assumption here is that more should be charged per hour for cars parked for a long time.

Charles Kepner and Benjamin Tregoe (2) developed a technique for solving problems which is used internationally. The problem is considered to be a deviation from the anticipated result and the technique is based upon a rational approach to problem-solving. In contrast, divergent problem-solving techniques encourage open thought and include:

- *Checklist*. A list of items can be drawn up to assist in the clarification of the problem or to help develop possible solutions.

- *SCAMPER*. Eberle (3) developed this acronym: substitute, combine, adapt, magnify (or minimize), put to other uses, eliminate or reverse.

For example a chef attempting to develop a range of low calorie menu items may be able to substitute high calorie ingredients with healthier alternatives.

- *Problem division.* Sometimes a problem can be divided into two or more dimensions. Each dimension can then be analyzed seperately. For example organizational communication problems could be analyzed by form e.g. verbal content of the message or direction of travel e.g. up, down and across the organization.

- *Brainstorming.* This is an idea generating technique which is used by groups. The principle of the technique is to allow as many ideas as possible to develop before any evaluation is undertaken.

- *Card writing.* With this approach individuals can prepare written suggestions and circulate them to other members of the group to refine or adapt.

It should be noted that creative thought can be hindered by conscious or unconscious constraints which people impose upon themselves. For example, a marketing manager in a brewery company may wish to adopt the same strategy to improve sales, which has been successful in the past, even though the problem is different. In other words the marketing manager does not search for a new solution. Creativity can also be stifled by the need to view processes as patterns i.e. individuals have expectations about the form the solution should take.

People do not usually like being identified as different from other members in their group and as a result there is a tendency for them to conform. This can lead to a lack of creativity and innovation in the organization. Sometimes there is an urgency to develop a solution to a problem before there is sufficient consideration of all the options available. Individuals may also be concerned about looking foolish when they propose ideas for solving a problem. Such worries obviously prevent the implementation of creative solutions.

Solutions can be developed at the individual or group level. Where groups are involved in problem-solving, it is important to appreciate that the group will have task and maintenance roles to perform. Task roles concern achieving the solution and maintenance roles concern managing the group members. A group takes time to become established and has to pass through a number of stages before it is working well. The key stages are:

- *Forming.* At this point group members are observing each other and identifying different styles of behaviour.

- *Storming.* Some conflict may arise between members and the leadership may be challenged.

- *Norming.* The group begins to work together and members support each other to achieve the task.

- *Performing.* The work is underway and the task is near completion.

It is essential that managers realize the importance of groups moving through the above stages. The urgency of a particular problem may encourage managers to move fast and demand a quick answer from the group. If the solution is to be successful it is important that enough time is given to the group processes.

It should also be appreciated that individuals play different roles in groups. For example the 'clarifier' will require individuals to be precise in their statements. The 'supporter' will offer help and encouragement and the 'observer' will identify any difficulties the group has in making progress.

Selecting, implementing and evaluating a solution
(A: 11 pp 190-192; D: 8 pp 131-132;
E :6 pp 157-158)
In choosing between possible solutions it is important to be objective and systematic. This means identifying possible constraints such as resources and predicting the likely effects of making a particular decision. It should be remembered that sometimes solving one problem can lead to the creation of another. There are a number of techniques which can be used to assist the selection of an optimum solution. The techniques include cost benefit analysis and critical path analysis. Whilst a solution should be relatively straightforward to implement if it has been carefully selected there may be resistance from some individuals in the organization. In order to avoid implementation problems occurring it is useful to prepare a written plan which can then be used to review the effectiveness of the solution.

Planning is a way of outlining different approaches to specific problems and plans should be both firm and flexible. There needs to be a degree of discipline to ensure the plan is implemented effectively but at the same time there must be an opportunity to gather and respond to feedback. When implementing the plan attention must be given to timing and working through unforeseen difficulties.

By stating objectives clearly at the beginning, there is a framework for monitoring and evaluating the plan. The solution should be reviewed in human, financial and physical terms in order to evaluate the overall success or failure of the decision.

CONCLUSION

Everyone encounters problems during the course of their daily lives. There are two approaches that need to be developed. Firstly, where possible, individuals should try to prevent problems occurring. In many ways prevention is better than cure as far as dealing with problems is concerned. Where problems do exist it is important that people learn how to manage them effectively. In essence there are six steps in the problem-solving process: (a) defining the problem; (b) gathering data; (c) developing options; (d) evaluating and deciding; (e) implementing and (f) gaining feedback.

It is important that sufficient time is given to thinking through problems and carefully planning solutions. By evaluating the success of the solution it is possible to learn and improve on the process in the future.

References:

1.   T. Rickards, *Creativity and Problem-Solving at Work*. Gower, 1990.
2.   C.H. Kepner & B.B. Tregoe, *The New Rational Manager,* Kepner Tregoe Inc; Princeton, NJ, 1981.
3.   R. Eberle, *Games for Imagination Development.* D.O.K Press, Buffalo, NY, 1972.

Review questions:

1.   Identify a problem in a hospitality or tourism organization with which you are familiar. Distinguish between the cause and effects of the problem using diagrams to facilitate the presentation of the information.

2.   Provide a short report outlining the techniques that managers could adopt to develop a more creative approach to the methods they use to solve problems.

3.   Identify three problems which occurred in your placement organization and discuss the extent to which they were successfully resolved.

EXTENSION

Read: Chapter 1 of *Hospitality Management: A Human Resources Approach* (G: 1 pp 1-25)

This chapter provides an overview of the hospitality industry which encompasses structure, environmental influences organizational goals, objectives and policy. The chapter begins with a discussion on the development of the hospitality industry and the extent to which it is unique. The structure and staffing of organizations is explored and the nature of the product is examined. The environmental influences which are beyond the control of the individual manager are then discussed.

Extension questions:

1.   Identify three problems which hospitality/ tourism managers have to deal with concerning the nature of their 'product'. Discuss the extent to which these problems are unique to the hospitality/tourism industry.

2.   With regard to the environmental influences affecting hospitality and tourism industries select four factors which are likely to pose problems for managers in the next five years and discuss how these problems should be approached.

3.   Discuss the problems which a hospitality/ tourism organization may encounter if it considers profitability to be its only criteria for measuring the effectiveness of its management.

Practical exercises:

Read the two case studies (E: 6 p 173) and answer the questions which follow:

1.   Select a problem that you feel you did not handle well whilst working in a hospitality or tourism organization. Analyze your approach to the problem and prepare a presentation highlighting the mistakes you made and the lessons you learnt from this experience.

2.   Arrange a group brainstorming session to discuss one of the following topics: (a) saving energy; (b) reducing labour costs or (c) increasing bar sales.

3.   Comment on how successful the session was and identify the requirements of an effective brainstorming exercise.

13
CONFLICT

INTRODUCTION

Conflict is a naturally occurring phenomenon that affects individuals, groups of people and organizational life. It is commonly associated with the tension which relates to the fundamental human characteristic of ambivalence. Individuals have the capacity to understand both sides of an argument and the emotional complexity to feel quite differently about the same person or situation within a relatively short period of time. Further, people are subject to competing internal drives, needs and aspirations which stimulate thinking and action in the form of behaviour. When individuals form part of a group in an organizational setting with its own agenda and particular blend of structure, rules, norms and management styles, the potential for conflict is greatly increased. .

Conflict in part at least, reflects the tension between the need for stability and the demands for adjustment and adaptation made by an ever changing external environment. External forces, such as market conditions, new technology and government policy can compel organizational change. In turn, this creates tension as people seek to establish the agenda for change, shaped by differing interpretations of the organizational and personal implications that arise. This chapter sets out to investigate the potential sources of conflict and the skills needed to manage conflict successfully.

In this chapter:
- Negative and positive conflict
  (E: 34 pp 603-605)
- Sources of conflict within the organization
  (E: 34 pp 604-606)
- The management of conflict (E: 34 pp 603-609)
- Skills for conflict management
  (C: 11 pp 266-295)

REVIEW

Negative and positive conflict
(E: 34 pp 603-605)
Managerial work routinely involves conflict resolution and so the skills needed to manage conflict constitute an important asset. Further, managers need to be able to discern between negative sources of conflict which are likely to have a destructive

outcome and positive sources arising from conflicting creative, innovative and change-related ideas and suggestions which can stimulate debate. Positive conflict can have an energizing effect, especially if opinions are discussed openly and the ensuing debate can be directed towards reaching a concensus on the best way forward.

Conflict that is badly managed can lead to a misuse of resources, increased hostilty, reduced trust, less openness and reduced likelihood of a group working together to achieve desired goals. Such negative conflict can in the case of individuals, result in denial and suppression of feelings, aggression, neurosis, depression, illness and absence from work. Employees, whose views or creative energy are suppressed by the organization, may, according to Argyris (cited in Hodgetts (2)) revert to immature behaviour reminiscent of childhood, as a way of dealing with the conflict.

Sources of conflict within the organization
(E: 34 pp 604-606)
Conflict arises in organizations when individuals or groups have needs which are not being met. This may be due to conflicting organizational needs and objectives or conflict with other groups within the organization or third parties such as customers, suppliers or shareholders. In general terms, shareholders are interested in maximizing return on investment and this expectation may bring them into conflict with a company's senior management. Shareholders may seek short-term profit maximization (possibly at the expense of long-term gain) to achieve higher share dividends whereas the company board may prefer to re-invest to secure development, growth and long term profitability.

The potential sources of conflict affecting organizations can be defined in relation to five broad categories: (i) structural; (ii) economic; (iii) environmental; (iv) cultural and (v) social. Further, in many cases sources of conflict overlap, producing a complex web of interrelationships which requires a well coordinated organizational response. The five categories are as follows:

(i) Structural.
(a) The objectives or mission statement of the organization; (b) the nature of decision-making and the extent of participation; (c) management style; (d) the effectiveness of channels of communication and extent of information sharing; (e) pay structures, working conditions, negotiating and bargaining procedures; (f) trade union activities; (g) the extent of role conflict and ambiguity; (h) changes in working practices; (i) the introduction of new technology.

(ii) Economic.
(a) The allocation and use of resources; (b) internal competition for resources; (c) restructuring and cost cutting (rationalization); (d) performance measurement; (e) quality assurance procedures (efficiency vs. effectiveness).

(iii) Environmental.
(a) Pollution controls; (b) conservation (e.g. green belt areas); (c) pressure group action (e.g. local community actions to restrict an organization's physical expansion); (d) conflict between private costs and benefits and social costs and benefits (e.g. the private activities of a fast food restaurant and its customers may lead to social costs if litter is dropped nearby); (e) conflicting demands of customers (e.g. whether to allow, ban or provide smoking areas on commercial airlines).

(iv) Cultural.
(a) The attitudes, values and beliefs fostered and promoted by management (which may be shared by some staff and resisted by others); (b) political dogma; (c) organizational traditions (enshrined in 'custom and practice').

(v) Social.
(a) The varying needs of different groups of the workforce (e.g. smokers and non-smokers); (b) conflict between different personalities and interest groups.

As the list illustrates, latent sources of conflict are deeply embedded in organizational life and can never be completely eliminated. Consequently, no skill is more important to managerial effectiveness than the ability to resolve conflicting thoughts and actions. Further, conflict resolution is an interpersonal skill that draws on many other interpersonal skills such as goal setting, listening, oral persuasion and feedback.

Formal goals, as well as guiding and motivating employees, help to prevent conflict by reducing ambiguity and sublimating personal interests to the needs of the organization. Goal setting creates performance standards so that the potentially destructive sources of conflict and associated behaviours become more visible and thereby easier to detect.

The ability to listen and provide constructive feedback help to ensure that communications are timely and accurate. If this one issue is effectively addressed (so that through its communications the organization promotes clarity of direction and purpose) conflict arising from misinformation can be contained.

Further, the use of informal channels for disseminating information orally throughout the organizational hierarchy can assist in promoting a less confrontational style of leadership. If informal channels can be established and maintained it will also encourage the use of oral persuasion, thereby enabling organizational goals to be achieved without the need to exercise formal authority. This approach would enable many differences of opinion to be discussed openly as and when they occur and differences resolved without excessive ill feeling or restment.

The management of conflict
(E: 34 pp 603-609)
There are two broad strategies for managing conflict:
- Maintain a focus on team building and turn negative conflict into positive action.
- Use one of five generic strategies to deal with conflict: (a) avoidance; (b) accommodation; (c) forcing; (d) compromise or (e) collaboration.

(a) *Avoidance.* Implicit here is a deliberate attempt to avoid facing conflict head-on. Avoidance is perhaps most appropriate when the conflict issue is trivial, when emotions are running high and time is needed mend relationships, or when the potential disruption from a more assertive action outweighs the benefits of resolution.

(b) *Accommodation.* This involves attempting to maintain a relationship by putting the other person's needs first. This strategy is most appropriate when the outcome of the dispute isn't personally important or significant, or if the aim is to re-establish a relationship, possibly with a view to gaining the person's support in resolving some other conflict or dispute.

(c) *Forcing.* This approach constitutes an attempt to satisfy personal objectives before those held by other parties to the dispute. This is likely to involve the use of power (the exercising of formal authority) to resolve the dispute. Forcing works well when a quick resolution is needed, on important issues where unpopular actions must be taken and where commitment by others to the proposed solution is not critical to its success.

(d) *Compromising.* In this instance all parties concede something so that a joint agreement can be reached. Compromising is most suited to situations where conflicting parties are about equal in power or status, when it is desirable to achieve a temporary solution to a complex issue or when time pressures demand an expedient solution.

(e) Collaboration. This approach aims to find a satisfactory (rather than optimal) solution for all parties involved in a dispute. It requires an honest and open discussion of the issues so as to ensure that a balanced and objective viewpoint is reached. Collaboration is the best strategy when time pressures are minimal, when all parties are seriously committed to a 'win-win' solution and when the issues under discussion are too important to compromise. Note: 'Compromising' and 'collaboration' are described by Evans (E: 34 pp 607-608) as *confrontation by negotiation.* He describes 'forcing' as *confrontation by the use of power.* He also refers to *avoidance* but instead of 'accommodation' refers to *defusion* (smoothing things over).

Skills for conflict management
(C: 11 pp 266-295)
The variety and complexity of conflict situations that can arise in organizations requires a structured and systematic response. A suggested approach involves six steps: (a) self-awareness; (b) selectivity; (c) evaluation; (d) analysis; (e) choice of strategy and (f) decision-making.

(a) Self-awareness. Individual differences account for the fact that managers attempt to resolve conflict in different ways. To some extent, this will depend on prior experience and managerial style, but it is also important to maintain a flexible approach so that the most appropriate solutions can be found. This requires a degree of self-awareness, sensitivity to the conflict situation and a willingness to adapt and learn from experience and from others.

(b) Selectivity. As noted above, a flexible and adaptable approach is a helpful starting point in resolving conflict. If this can be achieved, it is more likely that the decisions made will be based on a selective assessment of the arguments and facts which is both sensitive to the views expressed and appropriate to the situational needs and priorities.

(c) Evaluation. Selective assessment is linked to the ability to make an impartial evaluation based on the differing perspectives of the conflicting parties. It is therefore important that the evaluation is considered to be fair and consistent, even if the conflicting parties find it difficult to accept the decisions taken.

(d) Analysis. As noted earlier, conflicts have varying causes, but according to Robbins (2) they can be divided into three categories:
- *Communication differences.* Disagreements arising from semantic difficulties or misunderstandings, often related to conflict over roles, objectives, personalities or value systems.

- *Structural differentiation.* The division of an organization into departments, the establishment of hierarchies to coordinate them, together with the rules and regulations needed to make it function, create problems of integration that often result in conflict. Individuals disagree over goals, decision alternatives, performance criteria, and resource allocations.
- *Personal differences.* Conflicts arising from differences in personalities and value systems.

(e) Choice of strategy. It is important to keep an open mind regarding the means by which conflict is resolved so that the most appropriate strategy to use in any given situation is determined by the circumstances rather than pre-determined criteria.

(f) Decision-making. In deciding on the most appropriate option to implement, three factors should be considered:
- The importance of the conflict issue;
- Whether the relationship is important in the longer term;
- How quickly the conflict needs to be resolved.

All things being equal, if the issue under dispute is critical to success, collaboration is preferable. If maintaining stable and supportive relationships are more important the optimal strategies, in order of preference are: (i) accommodation; (ii) collaboration; (iii) compromise and (iv) avoidance. If it is vitally important to resolve the conflict as quickly as possible the most appropriate strategies are likely to be: (i) forcing; (ii) accommodation and (iii) compromise.

CONCLUSION

Conflict is an integral part of the human condition and therefore a natural aspect of organizational life. Every manager at some time or other will find him/herself in conflict with other managers at the same level or above. In addition, sources of conflict will need to be dealt with as a matter of routine within the team or group that they manage.

Successful hospitality and tourism organizations strive to establish a culture of continuous improvement and this means creating an environment that can absorb change and is capable of responding to turbulent market conditions. Unfortunately, change causes disruption and uncertainty. This can lead to resistance and conflict, thereby mitigating the potential benefits of change. In this respect, skilful resolution of ambiguity and conflict is needed and if the stategies employed are successful, they will also be instrumental in achieving further performance improvements.

References:

1.   Ernst & Young. *Employer Briefing*. Ernst & Young, London, Summer 1994.

2.   Hodgetts. *Organizational Behaviour: Theory and Practice*. Merrill, New York, 1991, pp 59-60.

3.   Robbins. *Training in Interpersonal Skills*. Prentice-Hall, London, 1989.

Review questions:

1.   Imagine that you are the supervisor of a team operating a large tour operator's computerized reservation system. You suspect that one of the team is taking drugs on the job, or at least is showing up for work under the influence of drugs. What would you do?

2.   A manager of a hotel company is meeting a group of shareholders who are unhappy about the low return declared on company shares. The manager has to convince shareholders that profit retention is necessary to support the future growth of the business. What should be the main points in the manager's argument, which interpersonal skills need to be used and how should he deploy them?

3.   An airline company manager is about to be promoted to a more senior position. A colleague who is also a personal friend, happens to know several things about the manager which, should management know, would make him unsuitable for the post. There is a conflict of loyalty. What should the friend do in these circumstances?

EXTENSION

Read: Chapter 34 of *Supervisory Management: Principles and Practice* (E: 34 pp 603-609)

As well as exploring aspects of conflict and strategies for responding to and dealing with conflict, this chapter encourages the reader to examine their own conflict-handling style. The following scenario provides an opportunity to explore a conflict situation.

Extension questions:
Scenario.
You are the general manager of a busy leisure complex with three deputy managers. The unwritten rule, relating to leave, is that no more than one member of the management team is away at any given time, due to the need to ensure duty management coverage throughout the day from 8am until 10pm. All three approach you with a leave request for the same two week period. Josie (single, and wanting to go on holiday with her boyfriend, is the most senior of the three); Chris (whose wife can only take these two weeks leave from her job) and Emma (who wants to attend a training course). Each of them hears of the others' application and a furious row breaks out. The atmosphere between them remains tense and action to resolve the conflict is needed.

As the manager you are considering the following options for dealing with the situation:
  (i).   Calling them together and explaining that they must sort the matter out themselves, otherwise none of them will be allowed to take leave at the requested time.
  (ii).   Talking the matter over with each of them separately. Making a decision as to whose need is most pressing, getting them all together and announcing a decision.
  (iii). Telling them individually not to be silly, and suggesting that they take some time to talk the matter over together.

1.   Identify the type of strategy implied by each of the above possible courses of action.

2.   Outline the pros and cons of each course of action.

3.   Consider how a team building approach might prevent problems like this arising in future.

Practical exercises:

1.   Explore the issue of personal responsibility for managing conflict by completing exercises 43, 44 and 45 (C: 11 pp 271-277). Form a small group to discuss your individual responses and report back to the tutor group.

2.   Examine how the development of certain teamwork skills in hospitalty and tourism settings can reduce the level of conflict by completing experiments 13 and 14 (C: 11 p 282 and p 294). Discuss your ideas in a small group and present your findings to the tutor group.

14
STRESS AND ANGER

INTRODUCTION

"Subjecting fewer managers to ever-larger workloads will only produce short-term benefits. Organizations in the 1990s risk burning out the very managers who are critical to the success of the organization." Roger Young, (*The Times,* 13/1/94, p. 18.)

According to the Institute of Management, the recession and resulting rationalization of organizations, have led to increased working hours and greater pressure for British managers. The result, according to their recent survey of 2,500 managers, was an increase both of 'stress and worry', on the one hand, and of 'pleasure and satisfaction' on the other. While the majority were positive about increased responsibility and workload, they felt that the extra pressure had occurred at the point in their lives when they also had the greatest family commitments. Many therefore experienced anxiety as a result of the ensuing conflicting demands placed on their time, prospects for career advancement and job security. ('Managers at their limits', *The Times,* p.18, 13/1/94, p. 18.)

It is vitally important for managers of hospitality and tourism organizations to be aware of how pressures can lead to stress and to learn techniques for the successful management of stress. This chapter seeks to address these issues.

In this chapter:
- What is stress? (A: 11 pp 178-201)
- The causes of stress
  (A: 1 pp 1-12; A: 2 pp 13-23)
- Stress and the workplace
  (B: 13 p 302; D: 6 pp 92-101)
- Stress and personality
  (A: 2 pp 13-23; A: 4 pp 41-56)
- Stress and anger
  (A: 11 pp 178-201; C: 10 pp 237-265)
- Management of stress and anger (A: 11 pp 178-201; C: 10 pp 237-265; C: 11 pp 266-296)(1)

REVIEW

What is stress?
(A: 11 pp178-201)
Stress is the pressure or sense of mental pain experienced when the demands on a person's mental and physical resources exceed their ability to cope.

Stress is manifested through bodily symptoms and changes in thoughts, feelings and behaviour. In moderation, stress can be beneficial - it can motivate and feel exhilarating. In excess however it can lead to physical and mental illness. Stress leads to increased secretion of chemicals known as 'glucocortoroids', which, while providing extra energy, suppress the immune system, thereby weakening the body's defences. At the same time a cocktail of hormones including adrenalin are released which while increasing mental alertness, triggers the liver to produce cholestrol. This can in excess, lead to the development of fatty deposits in arteries, raising blood pressure and increasing the possibility of a heart attack or stroke. Stress can also lead to the use of drugs such as alcohol and tobacco, which can themselves cause health problems.

The first signs of stress are usually feelings of *physical tension* - feeling worn out, physical complaints such as breathlessness, chest pains, palpitations, indigestion or a tight feeling in the stomach and *psychological problems* such as an inability to make decisions, being critical of others, being impatient, forgetful, irritable, nagging, or wanting to escape. The continuance of these symptoms of stress can lead to physical and mental exhaustion (burn out) with accompanying illness, fatigue and depression which in extreme cases, can lead to suicide.

The causes of stress
(A: 1 pp 1-12; A: 2 pp 13-23)
The way in which the individual experiences stress will depend on their perception of, attitude and response to, any stressful event or situation. The same event may bring pleasure to one person and stress to another. The ultimate answer to combating stress is therefore to adjust perceptions, attitudes and responses and to improve thinking skills. It should be noted however, that there are certain traumatic life events that cause distress such as the death of a close relative or friend, serious accidents or injuries, divorce, redundancy, bankruptcy. On a daily basis however, when faced with difficulties arising from personal relationships, work and the social environment, it is possible to react differently so as to minimize the incidence of stress.

There are two aspects of stress that are particularly relevant to the hospitality and tourism manager, first the workplace, and second, personality traits.

Stress and the workplace
(B: 13 p 302; D: 6 pp 92-101)
In England during 1993, there were at least four cases of employees suing their employers because of stress allegedly relating to the workplace. In one case, a former city worker claimed that a 10-15 hour working day had caused a breakdown in her health. Just as with asbestos, the issue of stress therefore looks set to have important legal and financial implications for employers and management in the future:

"Stress has further financial implications for employers due to sickness absence (recent Manchester University research showed that 90 million working days were being lost in the UK through stress) *and because staff experiencing stress will not produce their best work. Professor Robert Karasek of the University of Southern California studied several thousand employees in America and Sweden, and found that men whose jobs were demanding and lacking in autonomy were more likely to report depression, exhaustion and insomnia. They also took more sleeping pills and tranquillisers, and were off work more than men in less stressful jobs...and these problems were not caused by the men's personalities because when they changed jobs their symptoms improved."* Further, stress levels cannot simply be predicted by looking at job descriptions. In some jobs *"...the demands are high but so is the personal control."* In others *"...an apparently stressless existence...may actually be fraught...because of bad managerial policies, unreasonable or bullying superiors, poor communications and inadequate definitions of what different people's responsibilities are in the organization."* ('Why the office is no party', *The Times,* 28/10/93, p17.)

In hospitality and tourism organizations sources of workplace stress may arise from:

- *The working conditions.* Relatively low pay, and long hours, job uncertainty (casual labour), physically demanding working conditions (for example, heat in kitchens, smoke in bars) and the potential threat of exploitation arising from long hours of work and low pay.

- *Lack of career opportunities or discriminatory practices.* For example, lack of childcare arrangements for parents.

- *The service nature of the work.* The high expectations of customers and 'having to be nice all the time'.

- *Role ambiguity and uncertainty.* For example, a waiter may be asked to also help out in the kitchen or on reception or at the till, as well as serve food.

- *The organizational culture and climate.* The industry is traditionally renouned for its autocratic, bureaucratic and sometimes 'macho' style of working.

- *Limited opportunities for participation in decision-making.* The prevailing managerial style, limited availability of information the characteristically tight span of control and a reluctance to foster a climate of participation in decision-making can be contributory factors.

- *Changing work practices.* These are often linked to initiatives such as productivity improvement and the introduction of new technology.

If managers of hospitality and tourism businesses don't manage their human resources well, they risk loss of business. One important dimension of this is to reduce staff stress. Jobs need to be designed to enrich, and tasks should be varied in order to get the best out of people. Management by autocracy needs to give way to greater control and autonomy for staff. People need to be regularly rewarded and told they are doing a good job. Further, institutional stress factors need to be identified and either mitigated or eliminated.

There is evidence to suggest that managers can handle stress if they fully understand the circumstances that are causing it. For instance, eighty-three percent of managers felt that incompetent senior managers were one of the biggest sources of stress. ('Managers at their limits', *The Times,* p.18, 13/1/94, p. 18.) It may be necessary therefore, to employ specialist clinical psychologists to advise companies on how to instigate practices which minimize stress and maximize potential.

Stress and personality
(A: 2 pp 13-23; A: 4 pp 41-56)
Some personalities thrive on high-pressure jobs because of the exhilaration of the challenge; others wilt and burn-out under pressure. So, what is the link between stress and personality? Perhaps the most influential research done in this area was in the early 1960s by Meyer Friedman and Ray Rosenman.

They describe three personality types (*Types A, B and H*) in relation to: (a) characteristics and (b) relative stress levels.

(a) Personality characteristics.
Type A personalities are competitive, aggressive, tense, impatient, achievers, driven by the thought of success and very conscious of time. *Type B* personalities are more relaxed, better listeners, take time out and not generally slaves to deadlines.

(b) Relative stress levels.
Type A personalities experience a much higher rate of coronary heart disease. Among *Type A* personalities, a third category *Type H*, is identified. *Type H* personalities share three common characteristics; impatience (always hurrying), hostility (openly aggressive and/or angry) and little or no sense of humour (an inability to see the funny side of life or laugh at themselves). *Type H* personalities are particularly prone to stress-related illness and heart disease.

Personality *Type A, B, or H* characteristics can be identified by questionnaire. Findings can then be used as the basis for stress counselling with the individual being taught stress management techniques coupled with an appropriate means of monitoring progress.

Managers in hospitality and tourism organizations seeking to maintain the health and productivity of their staff are well advised to explore these and similar pro-active approaches to dealing with outbreaks of stress.

Stress and anger
(A: 11 pp 178-201; C: 10 pp 237-265)
Among the many stressful feelings that people experience, anger is possibly the most difficult to understand and cope with. Anger is an emotional reaction to the stress of provocation. Further, it is a two edged sword; on the one hand it fosters strength and a determination to take action and on the other, it can lead to irresponsible, irrational or even violent behaviour.

The positive side of anger is that it can constitute: (a) a signal that action is required; (b) a feeling of doing something; (c) a way of releasing tension and of communicating feelings to others and (d) a means of energizing the body's resources for self-defence.

The negative side of anger causes: (a) disruption to what are normally rational thought processes; (b) aggressive feelings and/or actions and (c) an unwillingness to face-up to a groundswell of negative emotions.

It is important to distinguish between *anger* and *aggression*. Anger evokes a *desire* for retaliation whereas aggression involves an *act* of physical or verbal hostility. The significance of this distinction is that an individual can be taught to handle anger and express it in ways that are not damaging to either themselves or others.

Anger becomes a problem when it occurs too frequently, when it is used unnecessarily, or when the feeling is too intense or sustained for too long. High levels of anger deplete the body in the same way as any other cause of stress and in this state of mind it is more likely to lead to aggression, disruptions and damaged relationships.

Anger is generally associated with an interaction of internal and external factors. External factors include provocations such as abuse, injustice, or unfairness. The occurence of anger is likely to depend upon the individual's perceptions and on how the perceived threat is processed. It also depends on what is commonly known as 'temperament'.

A debate exists as to whether anger is ingrained (natural occuring) or learned (nurtured). An individual's experience of anger depends on two internal processes. The first, *cognitive* processes, involves appraisal (whether the form of provocation is taken personally), expectations (of others) and self-talk (negative, neutral or positive). The second is the individual's *level of arousal* (how tense, agitated or upset the person feels).

The interaction between the individual's internal and external world leads to particular forms of behaviour, which in turn influence other peoples' reactions. Two styles of behaviour contribute to anger: (a) *withdrawal-avoidance* where nothing is done and the anger is turned inwards, thereby contributing to depression and (b) *antagonism-hostility-aggression,* where the individual acts in a way that is likely to stimulate further conflict.

Management of stress and anger
(A: 11 pp 178-201; C: 10 pp 237-265; C: 11 pp 266-296)(1)
Managing stress involves coping with pressures and demands of various kinds. Managing demand starts with learning how to perceive people and situations more accurately. It requires skills in assertiveness (particularly the ability to say no), negotiation, time management , personal organization, problem solving and decision-making. Further, it involves setting goals that are realistic and attainable and the ability to accurately evaluate the consequences of actions taken.

Second, managing one's personal resources involves maintaining good mental and physical health and building on personal resources by acquiring knowledge and skills that enhance the ability to cope with all kinds of life events. Health maintenance also includes balancing rest with appropriate exercise, attention to diet, treats, acquiring emotional control, and learning how to relax (using techniques like meditation, massage, rational-emotive therapy, relaxation tapes and bio-feedback). Third, managing anger involves taking action that is aimed at resolving a problem. The central skill in anger management is the ability to communicate feelings in an effective, non-hostile way. This requires: (a) the development of cognitive and emotional controls by understanding one's own, as well as other people's feelings; (b) using appropriate self-talk; (c) cultivating a sense of humour and learning to relax and (d) the development of behavioural controls by learning to communicate effectively, being assertive, and taking a task-oriented, problem-solving approach.

CONCLUSION

An awareness of the causes and effects as well as the mechanisms for managing stress are vitally important tools for hospitality and tourism managers. The ability to use these tools should also extend to strategies for devising and adopting suitable coping strategies. The ability to implementing appropriate procedures designed to monitor and reduce stress among the workforce can save money and time lost through absenteeism and low morale. Equally, a greater sensitivity to the forms of stress experienced by customers greatly facilitates the process of redesigning products or services and shaping environments which are conducive to customers who are purchasing and consuming hospitality and tourism products and services.

Reference:

1.   M.Watts & C. L. Cooper, *Dealing with Stress*. BBC books, London, 1992.

Review questions:

1.   What are likely to be the main causes of stress experienced by tourists on a foreign package holiday? How might the travel industry reduce the potential impact of stress?

2.   Consider the different ways in which hospitality/tourism managers can help their staff to manage anger and stress more effectively.

3.   Consider how the more positive aspects of stress might be used to good effect in the management of a theme park operation.

EXTENSION

Read: Chapter 6 of *People and the Hotel and Catering Industry* (D: 6 pp 90 -94)

This chapter includes a discussion of the problems that result from adopting roles. It considers for instance role ambiguity, role overload, and role conflict and looks at how to manage them and make them work more effectively in order to reduce stress in the workplace.

Extension questions:

1.   Identify the main role problems for staff working in: (a) a hotel; (b) a restaurant and (c) a commercial airline. How might such problems be managed and reduced?

2.   What are the most appropriate methods for monitoring staff stress levels in hospitality and tourism organizations?

3.   Are there any situations in the hospitality and tourism environment when it would be particularly appropriate for staff to adopt *Type A* behaviour in preference to *Type B* behaviour?

Practical exercises:

Undertake the following exercises, discuss your responses in small groups and after the session, evaluate your personal reactions:

1.   Assess your ability to manage anger by completing exercises 36-38 (C: 10 pp 241-249).

2.   Investigate your capacity to control anger by completing exercises 39-42 and experiment 12 (C: 10 pp 249-260).

3.   Complete: 'Thinksheet 48' (Using thinking skills to prevent problems in A: 11 p 183).

4.   Complete: 'Thinksheets 49-52' (in A: 11 pp 186-201). Evaluate your personal responses to questions 3 and 4 by means of the small group discussion.

15
ASSERTIVENESS

INTRODUCTION

"By learning to be assertive in our relationships we begin to take more control of our lives."
C.Walmsley (1).

Assertiveness is about developing relationships based on directness, honesty and respect, where communicating one's needs clearly to others and negotiating change, becomes a part of normal behaviour. In the hospitality and tourism industries assertion is an important interpersonal skill required to facilitate and enhance working relationships between employees, managers and staff, staff and customers, employees and external agencies.

This chapter examines the main principles of assertiveness using situations commonly found within hospitality and tourism organizations. Further it emphasizes the importance of becoming assertive as distinct from being either passive or aggressive. It should be noted however that though the literature gives guidelines on how to act assertively, such behaviour should be modified in practice to suit the needs, skills and personalities of particular individuals. In some situations it might for example, be more appropriate to be passive rather than assertive.

In this chapter:
- What it means to be assertive
  (A: 9 pp 148-149; C: 9 pp 210-213)
- Non-assertion (passive behaviour) aggression and assertion (C: 9 pp 212-219)
- Assertive thinking (A: 4 pp 51-53; A: 8 pp 113-128; A: 9 pp 206-211; C: 9 pp 212-236)
- Assertive behaviour
  (A: 9 pp 208-211; C: 9 pp 222-236)

REVIEW

What it means to be assertive
(A: 9 pp 148-149; C: 9 pp 210-213)
To become assertive it is necessary to examine ourselves and the way we relate to other people. This involves working on three interrelated areas.

The first is 'assertion for me' where the emphasis is on preserving my rights, meeting my needs and on expressing my positive and negative thoughts and feelings. The second area is 'assertion for you' where I endeavour to help you to assert and define yourself. The third area is 'assertion for us' where I am concerned also for the quality, health and vitality of our relationship.

Building an effective relationship entails developing on open communication system in which for the benefit of our relationship, we strive honestly and considerately to express our positive and negative thoughts and feelings and to act constructively towards each other.

Non-assertion (passive behaviour) aggression and assertion (C: 9 pp 212-219)
Behaving in an assertive manner involves acknowledging your own rights and the rights of others. Non-assertion, passive or repressive behaviour entails the denial of your personal priorities and rights. Aggression involves the denial of other peoples' rights: 'We shout, have rows...' (*Aggressive*) '...or quietly sulk or simmer with resentment if things don't go our way.' (*Passive*) (2)

Assertion means standing up for yourself and honestly expressing your feelings without either being inhibited or engaging in character assassination. Consider for example, a customer in a restaurant concerned about the way his bill has been calculated:

> *Passive:* Customer says nothing feels agitated and hastens out of the restaurant.
> *Aggressive:* 'Are you trying to pull a fast one? This bill's way over what it should be.'
> *Assertive:* 'I'm not clear how this bill has been arrived at. I would like you to explain, how you've arrived at this total.'

Positive thoughts and feelings may also be expressed in non-assertive, aggressive and assertive ways. For example, a waitress whose work was not up to standard has responded to advice and is now working effectively. The supervisor's response may be:

> *Passive:* Pleased but say nothing.
> *Aggressive:* 'Thats really good, about time you did something right!'
> *Assertive:* 'You're doing a very good job. Thanks a lot.'

Assertive thinking
(A: 4 pp 51-53; A: 8 pp 113-128; A: 9 pp 206-211;
C: 9 pp 212-236)
To develop effective relationships you need to assert yourself both inwardly and outwardly. Inner assertion involves acknowledging and working on those aspects of your inner self that weaken your effectiveness. This requires awareness of deficiencies in your present thinking skills and taking steps to improve them. Nelson-Jones (C: 9 pp 203-204) provides a checklist for assessing thinking skills which can be improved by: (a) attributing cause accurately; (b) using coping self talk; (c) choosing realistic personal and relationship rules and (d) accurately predicting gain and loss.

(a) Attributing cause accurately.
This involves realizing that you can misjudge the cause of a personal problem and perhaps fail to acknowledge your own part in the creation of the problem. For example, 'My essay-writing has always been bad and there's nothing I can do about it.' Such mis-attributions are unhelpful. It is better to consider the facts and formulate accurate attributions that enable you to develop and grow. For example, 'I've never really taken the time to learn the techniques of essay writing, I know I could improve if I did, and it's certainly in my interests to try'.

(b) Using coping self-talk.
This involves replacing negative self-talk with 'calming and coaching self-talk' (A: 12 p. 203). Talking to yourself in a negative way blocks your ability to be assertive and discourages you from taking action that might improve your life. For example: 'I'm just hopeless when it comes to talking to the opposite sex!'.

Calming self-talk involves the presence of supporting, and the absence of negative self-talk. For example, telling yourself to stay calm, 'slow down...you can cope!' *Coaching* self-talk involves clarifying personal goals, breaking tasks down and concentrating on the task at hand. For example, coping self-talk for a job interview:

> *Before:* 'Let's think through how I can best present my case. Relax! even if I don't get the job it's not the end of the world'.
> *During:* 'Speak firmly, but calmly and answer the questions asked. It's ok to be anxious, I know I can manage these feelings'.
> *After:* 'I did it. I managed to contain my negative ideas and got the job *or* even though I didn't get the job, I did well to be selected for the interview and I'm doing better each time'.

(c) Choosing realistic rules.
Choosing realistic rules requires becoming aware of sources of conflict and reformulating self-oppressing personal rules. Such rules may define ways of behaving based on age and gender stereotypes, family, cultural, or religious beliefs and peer pressure. These rules and accompanying behaviour may be unrealistic for you to live by and may prevent you from asserting your own needs and behaving in the manner that suits you. For example: 'Women should adopt the masculine stereotype in order to achieve' might be internalized as a personal rule. (see note below). A person who believes this and attempts to behave accordingly in order to achieve success may sacrifice or repress other fundamental needs in pursuit of the cultural stereotype.

Note: Findings presented to the British Psychological Society Conference in Birmingham in January 1994 by researchers from the University of Central London suggest that this is not the case: *"The typical male manager is extrovert dominant and adopts a tough poise but his female counterpart is likely to be quieter and more restrained as well as having better interpersonal skills"*. (Source: The Times 4/1/94.) Unrealistic personal rules must therefore be identified, questioned and reformulated into more effective working rules that help you develop and create effective relationships.

(d) Accurately predicting gain and loss.
An important prerequisite for assertive behaviour is the ability to accurately appraise the potential gains and losses of your actions. Predictions often contain perceptual distortions which lead to inaccurate assessments of risk and reward. Failure to predict reward accurately may discourage you from being assertive. Failure to predict risk accurately may cause you to be passive or aggressive, rather than being assertive. Accuracy in prediction can be improved by avoiding particular 'thinking errors' such as over-generalizing (i.e. drawing a broad conclusion from a specific observation). For instance: 'I am alone and unhappy now, so therefore I will always be alone and unhappy' and catastrophizing (i.e. making out that the negative consequences of not achieving your desired outcomes will be much worse than is justified).

Assertive behaviour
(A: 9 pp 208-211; C: 9 pp 222-236)
There are a number of related skills which constitute the basis of confident, assertive behaviour. These are: (a) verbal skills; (b) non-verbal skills; (c) the ability to handle power plays; (d) the ability to initiate change;

(e) the ability to request behavioural change; (f) the ability to end a relationship and (g) the ability to encourage others to be assertive.

(a) Verbal skills.
The *assertive* person talks in a clear strong and steady voice avoiding inappropriate anger or hostility, using words such as: 'I think' 'I want', 'we could' 'what do you think'. In contrast, the *non-assertive* person tends to giggle, whine, hesitate and use qualifying words such as 'maybe', 'would you mind very much?', 'I can't' or fillers such as 'you know' 'well' 'it's alright'. The *aggressive* person is more likely to be loud, jokey, explosive and use aggressive threatening words such as 'if you don't watch out', 'you must be joking' and 'rubbish'. For example, a barman has emotional problems. He comes into work persistently late, seems perpetually tired and his work suffers. The supervisor's response might be:

> *Non-assertive:* 'I know you've got problems but would you mind very much trying to get into work on time.'
> *Aggressive:* 'This just isn't good enough. If your work doesn't improve you're out.'
> *Assertive:* 'I want to talk to you about your work performance so that we can agree on a course of action to improve the situation.'

(b) Non-verbal skills.
Non-verbal skills also play a part in either reinforcing or negating the messages we are trying to convey. The assertive person will, for instance, maintain good eye contact and comfortable posture, and show sincere facial expressions. The passive person will be more prone to looking anywhere but at the other person, and fidget. The aggressive person is more liktely to glare, lean forward and use threatening gestures.

(c) The ability to handle power plays.
Handling power plays means having the courage to assert what you think without inhibition or aggression. You need to counteract not only the feelings within yourself, but also the messages from others. These 'dethinking' or 'put down' messages include advising, blaming, distracting, faltering, intellectualizing, intimidating, labelling, playing stupid, playing the victim, rule setting and talking down. To handle power plays effectively it is necessary to:
- Present a clear message;
- Persist in asserting what you think;
- Repeat the message;
- Stay calm;
- Stay focused on the main issue;
- Aim to negotiate solutions to end the interaction.

For example, a manager wishes to discipline an employee who continually leaves the hotel during working time without permission:

> *Manager:* 'You will recall that I've spoken to you on previous occasions about leaving the hotel during working time. I told you that you had to obtain permission from me before doing this, but I understand that you have chosen to ignore my warning.'
> *Employee:* 'Well I was only gone a short time. It didn't seem worth bothering you about it.'
> *Manager:* 'It is always worth bothering me about it. It is a rule of the organization that anyone leaving the hotel has to obtain the permission of the manager. This is the third occasion you have broken that rule.'
> *Employee:* 'It was just one of those things. The wife rang in, needed picking up from work, I had a slack period, you know how it is.'
> *Manager:* 'I have given you two verbal warnings to date on this matter, and this is my final one. Should you repeat this behaviour again, I will have no option other than to start a formal disciplinary procedure.'
> *Employee:* 'Oh come on now. I've worked here a long while, always given good service. We all make a few mistakes don't we?'
> *Manager:* 'I am going to make a note in your personal file that states if your break this rule again I will instigate formal disciplinary procedures. I suggest, therefore, that you heed this formal warning and seek my permission should you need to leave the hotel during working time.'

(d) The ability to initiate change.
Assertion involves initiating change and assuming responsibility for making things happen rather than waiting for the other person to make the first move. For example, hotel manager to supervisor:

> *Non-assertive:* 'Do you feel like helping me devise a new marketing strategy for the hotel?'
> *Aggressive:* 'You've got to pull your finger out and come up with some good ideas for marketing this hotel or we're in trouble.'
> *Assertive:* 'I would like to devise a new marketing strategy for the restaurant. Do you want to be involved?'

(e) The ability to request behavioural change.
Assertion may involve requesting a new behaviour or requesting more or less, of an existing behaviour. For example, a chambermaid cleaning bathroom mirrors regularly fails to wipe the mirror with a clean dry cloth and leaves smears on the mirrors.

The supervisor wants to stop this behaviour:

Non-assertive: Says nothing but gets increasingly irritated.

Aggressive: 'You're supposed to be cleaning the mirrors not making them even more filthy.'

Assertive: 'I am concerned that the mirrors are not being cleaned to standard. In future, I want you to use a separate clean dry cloth to finish each mirror.'

(f) The ability to end a relationship.
To end a relationship effectively requires assertion as distinct from passivity or aggression. It is necessary to be clear about what is needed, then apply the skills of assertion to negotiate the ending of the relationship. It is important not to assume responsibility for the other person, accept that some confrontation may be inevitable and show respect for yourself as well as the other person.

(g) The ability to encourage others to be assertive.
Assertive thinking and behaviour should recognize that other people need to be assertive too. Moreover, if we wish to develop a relationship with them we need to accommodate and encourage their assertiveness.

CONCLUSION

In essence, hospitality and tourism organizations employ people to provide services to other people. Assertiveness is one of the essential interpersonal skills required to ensure that this happens in an efficient and effective manner. It is based according to Walmsley (1) on self-esteem, self-knowledge, respect for others, and 'clear communication' and involves six steps (C: 9 p. 222): awareness; specifying goals; developing a plan; rehearsing; implementing your assertion; practicing and evaluating.

References:

1. C.Walmsley, *Assertiveness - The Right to Be You.* BBC Publications, London 1991.

2. S. Helmstetter, *What to Say When You Talk to Your Self.* Thorsons, London, 1986.

Review questions:

1. Comment on the importance of assertiveness for the hospitality and tourism industries.

2. Consider the relevance of the principles of assertion to the marketing of services.

3. Analyze the political and socio-economic implications of assertiveness training programmes for minority groupings in society.

EXTENSION

Read: Chapter 4 of *Lifeskills A Handbook* (B: 4 pp 69-79)

This chapter examines the design of life-skills training programmes. It takes skill assertiveness as an example to illustrate the format for training programmes. The chapter should prove useful to anyone working in the hospitality or tourism industries who is asked to design or participate in such a programme. Further, it provides background to the first extension question.

Extension questions:

1. Imagine you are the personnel director of a large hotel chain. You have been asked to organize a series of workshops to train staff in the skills of assertiveness. Each workshop is to last a day. Draw up a schedule of the days activities, with a brief description of what each activity would entail.

2. To what extent do organizational structures and management styles discourage assertive behaviour by staff?

Practical exercises:

1. Read: (C: 9 pp 233-234). Write down the main considerations for ending a relationship assertively. Discuss you views in a small group setting.

2. Imagine you are a manager working in a hospitality or tourism organization of your choice. From time to time, you have to discipline members of staff. Do you think that you would be influenced by any special sex-role or cultural considerations in how you might discipline staff? If so, how would these issues influence your approach? Discuss you views in a small group setting.

3. Make notes on the key requirements relating to assertion most relevant to chairing a meeting. Working in a small group, formulate an 'ideal' set of characteristics and behaviours for this task.